TRACING THE HISTORY OF VILLAGES

Trevor Yorke

COUNTRYSIDE BOOKS
NEWBURY, BERKSHIRE

First published 2001
© Trevor Yorke 2001

COUNTRYSIDE BOOKS
3 Catherine Road
Newbury, Berkshire

To view our complete range of books,
please visit us at
www.countrysidebooks.co.uk

ISBN 1 85306 712 1

Designed by KDP, Kingsclere
Maps, photographs and illustrations
by the author

Produced through MRM Associates Ltd., Reading
Printed by J.W. Arrowsmith Ltd. , Bristol

CONTENTS

INTRODUCTION

The English Village. Just mention these three words and you probably conjure up images in your mind of winding lanes bordered by rustic stone cottages and black and white half-timbered houses, framed by picket fences and mighty oaks. Most people would include a church in their imaginary composition, not too large but with a tower or spire, some perhaps a farmyard with a tumbledown barn and livestock roaming free, while to others the view would not be complete without a local shop, its tingling bell upon entry inviting you into an amazing den of every imaginary necessity. In the foreground there would be the velvet lawn of the village green entertaining a game of cricket while the crowd cast an occasional eye then return to their pints outside the obligatory pub! It is a tranquil scene, the silence being only politely interrupted by the sound of leather on willow and the ringing of church bells while under the summer sun the smell of freshly cut grass and pungent flowers fills the nostrils.

This is the very image which soldiers in the First World War were sent to swell their patriotic hearts, which was stylised on 1920s posters selling the attributes of new suburban estates, and which enticed the working class invasion of the countryside by train and bicycle in the following decades. To the present generation countless television detectives programmes, period films and glossy magazines have crystallised this image of a rural heaven, its timeless and communal harmony striking a particular chord with urban dwellers dismayed by the pace of modern life and the loss of the community. As for me, my friends and I all aspire to own a cottage in the country while the villages of the Cotswolds, Devon and Cumbria have been the destination for endless holidays.

It was while on one of these breaks, on a particularly rainy Lake District day spent running between shops in Keswick, that I came across a book, *Roads and Tracks of Britain* by Christopher Taylor. I was curious about a Roman road which ran across the fell tops in the area where we were staying although I think the purchase was more influenced by the attractive rural scene on the front cover! Although primarily about transport it ended up shattering my understanding of the English village.

I had been taught at school about small groups of warlike prehistoric men living in huts beside long distance trackways until they were replaced by the refined Romans and miles of dead straight roads. When the Romans had gone our Saxon forefathers selected the best land and cut hamlets and lanes out of the primeval forest until after years of gradual growth when nothing much happened except the Black Death, the present traditional village emerged. Yet here was an author describing a very different landscape and history based upon the finds of modern archaeology, aerial photography and research. It was a manmade countryside, tamed in prehistory with fluctuating fortunes for those people who had shaped it over thousands of years. The villages, which the roads and tracks linked, developed and declined in all periods and all areas, with no generalisation of how this occurred being possible. They may have been created only a hundred years ago or could even have their origins in the Iron Age!

The curiosity which these revelations generated enticed me to research more of the books by today's experts in the field although I found many of them assumed the reader had a good background knowledge of the subject and terms used. I was also surprised how this new understanding of local history had not filtered down to the general public. It was these facts which inspired me to write *Tracing the History of Villages*, in a form that would bridge the gap between our school textbooks and the works of these experts, and as an introduction to the subject for the many people who want to begin researching the history of the village they live in.

You may share with me a frustration with village history books which spend most of their time listing countless lords of the manor, while what we are really interested in is what the village looked like, not which Frenchman owned it! I'm far more curious about the physical remains of hillforts, ridges and furrows, old castles, moats and ancient tracks than in pages of Latin text. I have therefore tried within this book to paint a picture of the physical appearance of villages in the different periods rather than concentrating on their social and economic history. The book is also packed with illustrations and photographs which show features as they would have originally appeared and then at the end of each chapter as you may still find them in or around your own village today.

The chapters cover five periods in history, the dates of which are not intended to represent any significant change or event. At the beginning of each one there is a view and description of an imaginary village which is intended to give a feel for the rural landscape at the time rather than a definitive record of a particular part of the country. There is also a chart with a line showing the approximate national population, though not with any specific figures as it is mainly intended to show that our history has been a roller-coaster ride rather than a steady progression. Within the chapters I have worked from an overall picture down to the individual elements of the village in that period. This covers some of the national events that affected village life, how agriculture and industry which the villages relied upon was developing and descriptions of the buildings, roads and people that formed it. The final chapter is for those who wish to trace the history of a specific village, listing areas to start your research, books which may help and places to visit.

Trevor Yorke

CHAPTER 1
EARLY SETTLEMENTS

The Prehistoric, Roman, and Early Saxon Period: 10,000 BC to AD 700

■ *FIG 1.1: The above illustration shows the area of our imaginary village around the time of the birth of Christ. In the foreground is a humble farmstead while on the hill beyond is a hillfort which acts as a market centre and a place for protection in times of trouble. Yet where are the primeval forests and men in animal skins that we were told about in school? This looks like an organised landscape and not a scattering of huts cut out of the heavily wooded valleys. This chapter will explain how modern archaeologists believe settlements and the landscape developed in this pre-medieval period and the influence they may have had on later villages.*

CLIMATE AND GEOLOGY

In our modern world where we can control our surroundings and assume a certain security against acts of God we forget the devastation which climatic and geological changes can cause. This was especially true in this prehistoric period. Climate is important to the village in its effect upon agriculture. Archaeologists can work out from various sources, including snail shells, pollen, seeds and the study of tree ring growth, whether man was expanding his holdings or abandoning them thousands of years ago. It is probable that these ups and downs which they have recorded were dependent on whether the climate was favourable or not at the time. In later periods we know that this was the case as deteriorating weather was one of the causes of village desertion especially on marginal lands in the 14th and 15th centuries. It is likely that much of our present day moorland as well as peat bogs were created by the clearing of woods, creation of fields and then their abandonment even as far back as the Bronze Age. Dartmoor is littered with abandoned settlements from this date and as late as the 13th century before the weak soils could support farming no more.

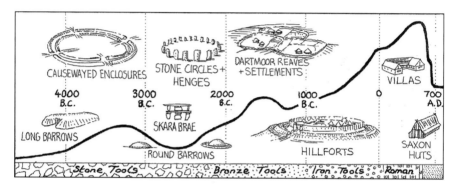

■ FIG 1.2: Although the line through this chart represents the possible population levels in this period, it reflects more the variations in climate and the effect it has been discovered to have on the settlements of the time. At its peak in the Roman period the population is generally agreed to be 4-5 million.

Another important area affected by both climatic and geological forces is rising and falling sea levels. Throughout time, changes in the climate have caused the ice caps to melt, raising the sea, and then allowed them to re-freeze, causing the level to drop. Geology has further confused this picture in Britain. The land is not as solid as we assume, it is made up of drifting continental plates and the very rocks of which they are composed can actually flow. After the last Ice Age the huge weight of the melting ice sheets was lifted from the north of Britain causing it to rise while as a reaction the south of the country lowered, making it appear that the sea level has risen in the South and dropped in the North.

The effects of these events can be seen all around our coastal regions with villages vanishing under the sea while in other parts it has retreated, leaving settlements which relied on coastal trade miles inland. The silting up of rivers, harbours and estuaries has also resulted in the transformation of once prosperous ports into peaceful villages, today surrounded by farmland. The actual geological composition of the cliffs can also determine how quickly the force of the sea can erode the coastline and plunge houses into its frothy jaws.

The development of your village will also be affected by the geology beneath it. The type of soil and its ability to drain water can determine whether crops are grown, livestock grazed or woodland planted upon it, while the local stone or lack of it will affect the buildings in the village itself. Although Chapter 2 will explain that our forefathers did not simply pick the best land for their settlement, certain sites have always been more attractive than others due to their geology. For instance on the dry chalk hills of the Downs and Chilterns, there are villages all along the springline where the water rushes out from the lower slopes. An understanding of these geological and climatic events which have in the past or still today affect your village is important before looking at how man has shaped the landscape and the settlement.

HUNTER GATHERERS

Around 12,000 years ago the last Ice Age was drawing to a close, and as the climate warmed Hunter Gatherer tribes moved up from the continent into the newly formed forests. These Mesolithic people would have probably established a main settlement, quite often near a shoreline or river, from which hunting parties would have ventured out to form temporary camps closer to their prey. Others in the community may have set up a seasonal base nearby from which to gather fruits and nuts.

In winter back at the base camp, best imagined as a group of wigwam-type tents, they would have relied on fishing to survive. These are no forebears of our villages, yet towards the end of this period there are increasing signs that these people were managing their environment, clearing areas of forest, perhaps to make hunting easier or even for early husbandry. They also appear to have traded, as stone from Dorset has been found as far away as Gloucestershire and Surrey. Perhaps it was this travelling which brought them into contact with people from the continent whose lives revolved around a new idea: farming.

AGRICULTURE

Whether it was an influx of the new farmers from Europe or just the existing people adopting their ways is unknown, but from around 4500 BC fields and crops appeared on the landscape. These Neolithic people are known to have grown wheat and barley, while in later periods rye, oats, spelt, and flax were also to be found. Fruits included crab apples, dwarf cherries and wild plums, while livestock comprised cattle, sheep, goats and pigs. Domesticated dogs possibly appeared before agriculture developed while the horse was a later arrival from 2000-1100 BC. It was during this period that the landscape of irregular shaped fields was being replaced by sometimes complex networks of rectangular ones which by the Iron Age had left us with possibly less woodland than today!

The effect of the arrival of the Romans in AD 43 was not to physically change this intensely farmed landscape but to refine the system. Firstly with technological improvements, notably the plough, which helped achieve higher yields, then secondly by putting in place an economic structure, a transport network and a ready market for the surplus agricultural produce. This success and stability can be seen in Fig 1.2 where our population line reaches its peak.

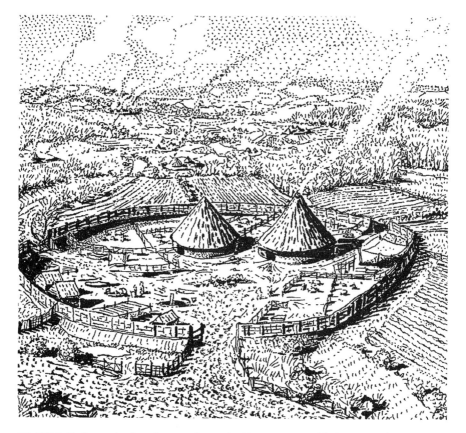

■ *FIG 1.3: An agricultural scene from the Bronze Age with farmsteads scattered in a landscape of small, lightly ploughed fields and surrounding woodland.*

When the Roman legions left these shores in AD 410 there was no great collapse in the system of farming. The remaining population, which must have still numbered in millions, and the incoming Saxons, more likely in just thousands, continued to use the existing fields during these so called Dark Ages. If you assume that the transition to a mainly Anglo Saxon kingdom was a relatively peaceful one then it is not impossible that some estate boundaries laid out in Iron Age or Roman times may have survived, possibly in the form of a parish boundary, around your village today. Yet as most of England's fields have since been reorganised by an open field system and then enclosure acts you are unlikely to find them still used in landscape today, except perhaps in areas like Devon where these later changes had little effect. It is also in counties like this that some of the physical remains of prehistoric field systems have survived where there has been no subsequent ploughing. Occasionally they can be seen on the ground like the 'reaves' on Dartmoor, but usually only from the air where great networks have been identified from Dorset and Devon up to Lincolnshire and Yorkshire.

VILLAGES

Villages were not the main type of rural settlement in England in prehistoric times. Even under the Romans it was a network of towns, hamlets and farmsteads that dominated the countryside. Where groups of people did gather in sufficient numbers for it to be termed a village, they tended not to stay very long. Perhaps limited agricultural techniques leading to soil exhaustion or simply a rudimentary belief that permanent occupation encouraged disease meant they chose a new site sometimes after only a few generations. This mobility is of note for should you discover that there was perhaps an Iron Age hamlet or a Roman villa under your present village it does not mean there has been continuous settlement on that site.

What is notable especially by the Iron Age is the density of the villages, hamlets and farmsteads. In the majority of England there is a good chance there will be far more of these prehistoric and Roman sites in your parish than current settlements. Over much of the Midlands and the South, sites were only a kilometre apart while even in the upland regions they were often within 2 or 3 kilometres of each other. Have a look at an OS Landranger map today which is marked out in kilometre squares to grasp how intensely packed this landscape was. Despite the rarity of villages, archaeologists do find examples all across the country, and at some of the more famous sites you will not require a trowel to appreciate them.

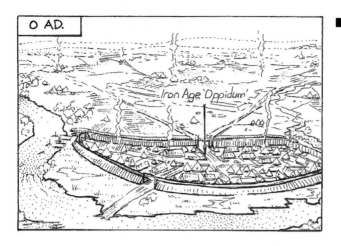

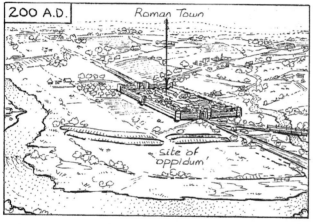

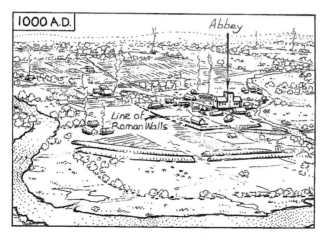

■ *FIG 1.4: DORCHESTER, OXFORDSHIRE: Three successive views showing how settlements can move over time within an area. The first shows the Iron Age oppidum near the river, while in the second, Roman, scene it has been replaced by a small walled town further north. In the final view the Saxon abbey and its dependent village have developed to the east of the Roman settlement. Today the banks of the oppidum, the line of the Roman town walls and the old abbey can still be seen.*

■ *FIG 1.5: SKARA BRAE, ORKNEY MAINLAND: One of the excavated houses with, to the left, a stone dresser to display prized possessions, towards the bottom the rectangular hearth and below the figure on the right the stone slabs which formed a box-shaped bed! Although it is not representative of houses from this period in England, it does show the level of refinement which could be achieved by early man.*

On the west coast of the Orkney Mainland, below Skaill House stood a number of sand dunes, one of which was known as Skara Brae. On a winter's night in 1850 a vicious storm ripped the turf from this particular dune and exposed stone walls of houses set in decomposed waste known as midden. The local Laird excavated the site and slowly uncovered four houses, complete with stone furniture, yet it was not until 1930 that the full extent of what is now termed a village was revealed. There were ten circular structures huddled together and linked by passages, the great age of which was not realised until modern scientific methods dated it to 3000 BC!

On Dartmoor there are literally hundreds of later Bronze Age hut circles, a few of which seem to have gathered into larger settlements. Riders Rings, near South Brent, has 36 dwellings which, although they did not all stand at the same time, formed a village that may have continually supported a population of up to a hundred. These sites survive because they were partly built with stone and the areas were not ploughed or built on in later times.

In the rest of England the settlements which we know existed have left little trace. The timbers of their houses have rotted away to leave just post holes and ditches which are only revealed by air photography or excavation. One notable site is Flag Fen, near Peterborough, where under a later Roman road a Bronze Age village of rectangular timber houses was found on an artificial island!

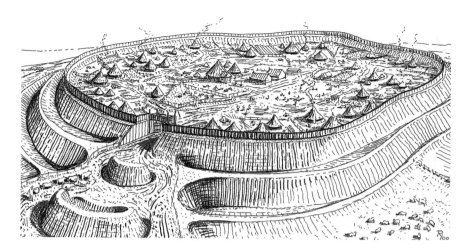

■ *FIG 1.6: A view of an imaginary hillfort of the later Iron Age with a more complex arrangement of gateway defences and outer ditches than on earlier forts.*

By the early Iron Age the pressure for land had led to the development of a type of settlement we know as the hillfort. These acted as centres of territories where produce was brought perhaps as a tribute or to be bartered with for other goods. They were also a place for protection for the surrounding dependent farmsteads in times of trouble, which perhaps occurred less often than was previously believed in spite of the sometimes mighty defences. In some forts grids of streets and houses have been uncovered, an obvious case of planning which is a theme that can occur in villages during any period.

Despite their role being more comparable to a town, the hillfort is the earliest relative of a village which you can see in the landscape today without excavation. This type of Iron Age settlement though was not dominant in all regions. In the east of the country, large open villages seem more common, while in the north-east small, ditched enclosures were the norm.

When the Romans arrived in AD 43 they did little to change the hamlets and villages of the indigenous tribes but introduced new settlement types, the architecture from which would later influence even the most remote parts of the country. The regional variation mentioned above became more simplified in the Roman period and can be crudely divided into an upland and lowland division as shown in Fig 1.7. Generally the lowland area was dominated by villas, which could vary from large palatial buildings with courtyards and gardens, down to small rectangular houses with just seven or eight rooms. At their height they controlled great agricultural estates, taking a role similar to an 18th or 19th century country house, with the workers usually living in settlements close to the villa. There were villages all over this region, not enclosed as in the previous millennia, but open, sometimes scattered or linear, along a road or track. Some were part of the villa or agricultural estates, while others developed to serve passing travellers or the military. There were also industrial settlements which formed around quarrying, iron workings, and brick, tile and pottery production, although these like their modern counterparts could be of a temporary nature.

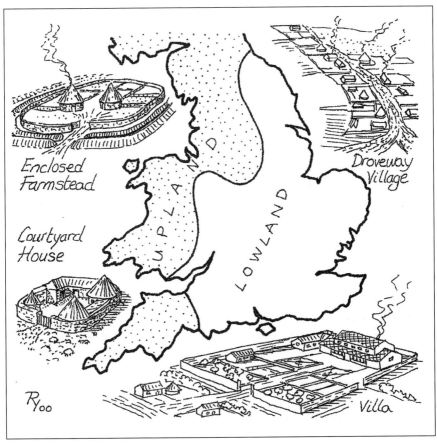

■ FIG 1.7: A map of England and Wales showing the approximate split between the lowland and upland regions with sketches of the types of settlement that could be found there in the Roman period.

In the upland zone, smaller enclosed farmsteads and hamlets were the most common, occasionally large enough to be termed a village. In the north they comprised circular houses surrounded by a ditch and bank or a stone wall while in the south-west slightly different types known as 'rounds' and 'courtyard houses' were widespread. Chysauster, four miles north of Penzance, is a famous example of the latter. Finally in both regions there were 'vici', civilian settlements which were established outside military forts where soldiers could shop, drink or pray. Towards the end of the 4th century there was probably a lot of the latter going on as the Roman political system collapsed and the army withdrew to the continent.

Yet after the final break in AD 410 there is little evidence for the traditional picture of Germanic armies marauding across the country and burning down the Britons' villages. The incoming Angles and Saxons did establish new settlements, mainly in eastern England and after AD 450, but these seem scattered, formless collections of timber huts and were only used for a number of generations. At West Stow, six miles north-west of Bury St Edmunds in Suffolk, there is a

■ *FIG 1.8: WEST STOW, SUFFOLK: An early Saxon village which dated from AD 400-650 was discovered on this site. As only the remains below ground (post holes, trenches and collapsed floors) were uncovered, the subsequent reconstructed buildings in the picture are experimental but still give a good idea of what the first Germanic settlers' houses would have looked like.*

reconstruction of one of these early villages. In the upland regions there seems little change until the 8th century except for those settlements which were dependent on the Roman military presence, where general abandonment is indicated from archaeology and a reduction in crop pollen.

Out of the mists of these still Dark Ages, new villages, some of a more familiar 'nucleated' form, appeared. At the centre of them, and possibly their reason for being, was the church.

RELIGION

The most commonly found and easily recognisable parts of prehistoric society in our landscape today are the remains of their religious endeavours. Long before churches were the focus of a village's Christian devotion, mysterious and powerful beliefs inspired people to construct henges, temples and barrows. When Neolithic man constructed Silbury Hill in Wiltshire, steps of chalk blocks and rubble were progressively built up over a staked out mound of clay and gravel, and then the 130 ft mound was finished off with a chalk 'icing'. The gleaming white pinnacle, the largest manmade mound in Europe, covered five and a half acres and took an estimated 1,000 labourers seven years to build!

Just up the road is Avebury, a present-day village set within a Neolithic stone circle, which is 1,435 ft in diameter and encloses 28 acres. The ditch alone required 200,000 tonnes of chalk to be dug out, while more than a hundred huge sarsen stones from the local fields had to be dragged into position. These projects clearly required great organisation which implies a social structure and large numbers of people with enough free time away from farming duties to build and maintain them. These religious centres though were not built for a village, nor were villages arranged around them like later churches. They served perhaps a tribe spread out in hamlets and farms.

The roots of our English churches lie not in these times but with the later introduction of Christianity to our shores. It first appeared in the 4th century after the Emperor Constantine was converted, but the collapse of Roman rule after AD 410 and the incoming heathen Germanic population saw the fledgling religion pushed into the west. Here a number of villas are believed to have become monasteries especially in South Wales and the South West and early churches are also known to have been founded. The conversion of the Anglo Saxons started with the arrival of the missionary Augustine in AD 597 and during the following century a 'Roman' church was established in England though sometimes at odds with the 'Celtic' church which had returned from Ireland and established itself in the north.

■ *FIG 1.9: AVEBURY, WILTSHIRE: Part of the stone circle which was in use from 2500-1600 BC. Many stones were destroyed by farmers during 17th century improvements to the land, it is believed by lighting fires under the stones, then pouring cold water over them until they cracked and could be broken up by hand.*

The ecclesiastical system at this time was one centred around minsters. These could be impressive stone structures with tall naves and chancels but usually no tower. A few survive in part today with Brixworth in Northamptonshire being a good early example, while a more humble church of this date can be found at Escomb in County Durham. From these centres the clergy would venture forth into the countryside and preach in villages and hamlets usually at a spot marked by a cross; there were no local vicars or parish churches.

■ *FIG 1.10: An Early Saxon church based on the existing church at Escomb in County Durham which dates from this period. Note the thatched roof and white walls.*

HOUSES

It is a fair generalisation to say that most pre-Roman houses in England were round ones. These were not flimsy mud huts though; by the Iron Age we find sturdy, well-designed structures that would long outlast the type of medieval peasant houses which appear some 1,500 years later! In the lowlands an outer ring of timber uprights would have wickerwork plaited between them and then daubed with a mix from mud, clay, chalk, straw, animal hair and blood. An inner ring or central post would take most of the weight of the immense low hanging thatched roof while some had an outer ring ditch which would act like a modern gutter in collecting rain water and protecting the foundations. A gap in the apex of the roof would let smoke from the hearth out, but the interiors must have been sooty and dim with no windows and only one door in all except the largest houses.

In the uplands there were similar types except that the roof could have been covered with heather and turf while the walls were built from stones. These could be surprisingly complex, for instance with inner and outer rings of larger boulders between which was a rubble core, similar to a dry stone wall today. Like their modern-day counterpart they could last a long time without maintenance and literally hundreds of hut circles, albeit in a collapsed form, are sprinkled over Dartmoor, some 3,500 years old!

■ *FIG 1.11:*
A Bronze Age hut of a type which stood on Dartmoor 3,000 or more years ago, with a cut out to show the elements in its construction.

Although the round house survived well into the first millennium AD in upland areas, the arrival of the Romans led to a gradual conversion to a rectangular form of house in the majority of villages in England. These would have used the same locally available materials as their predecessors, with only the more important houses like the villa using tiles and brick.

The early Saxon villages seem to comprise unfamiliar structures types, the most hotly debated ones being 'sunken featured buildings' (previously called 'sunken huts' or 'grubenhauser'). These are set over a pit with two uprights at each end supporting a ridge pole, very much like a traditional tent. The contentious point is whether the floor was raised above a pit used for storage or was the bottom of the pit the actual floor level? Whichever the case it is likely that these were workshops rather than houses. Elongated wooden buildings with walls of vertical timber, referred to as 'halls', were probably residential. It should also be remembered that the early Saxon settlers did not reach the upland areas of England where a continuation of the Romano British house types is likely.

■ *FIG 1.12: An imaginary Early Saxon village, with various forms of buildings as they may have appeared including the sunken huts to the middle right of the picture.*

TRANSPORT

The final and perhaps most surprising aspect of prehistoric England, which will clear your mind of any lingering misconceptions of our ancestors as primitives, is their communications network. We have evidence from way back in the Neolithic period of trading over great distances. Stone axes from the Langdales in the Lake District have been found as far away as Suffolk, while flints and pottery have also been discovered sometimes hundreds of miles from their source.

It is best to imagine the routes the early traders would have trodden as wide, unenclosed strips of land rather than the defined tracks which, for instance, the prehistoric Icknield Way is today. It is also important to note that there is no direct evidence for these ancient routes. In some cases early archaeologists simply linked the then limited number of known prehistoric sites on a map and

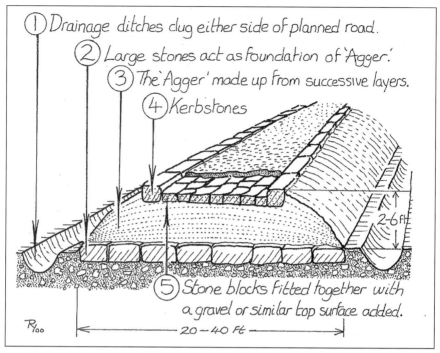

① Drainage ditches dug either side of planned road.

② Large stones act as foundation of 'Agger.'

③ The 'Agger' made up from successive layers.

④ Kerbstones

2-6 ft

⑤ Stone blocks fitted together with a gravel or similar top surface added.

R/∞

←———— 20 ~ 40 Ft ————→

■ *FIG 1.13: A section through a main Roman road showing the order from 1 to 5 of its construction.*

imagined a route between them. In the light of the huge number of settlement sites which have since been discovered it would be best to see any of these long distance routes as part of what must have been a large network of tracks. Only in exceptional circumstances have actual trackways survived like the famous Sweet Track in the Somerset Levels which was made of angled poles supporting a planked walkway, this particular one dating back to 4000 BC!

By the Iron Age we were trading with the continent from ports like Hengistbury Head, near Bournemouth, from where agricultural produce, minerals and slaves were exported in exchange for wine and exotic goods. We therefore had boats and carts to transport these goods and although the tracks were still unsophisticated there were bridges. One such one dating from the Bronze Age was recently discovered across an old course of the River Thames near Eton.

It was probably the presence of valuable minerals and agricultural surplus which first attracted the Romans to our shores. They brought with them surveyors and engineers who built the familiar straight roads, with ditches either side of a raised bank known as an agger, and a metalled surface laid on top. Unlike prehistoric tracks we can be more certain of the routes of these main Roman roads from existing earthworks, Old English names like 'Straet' and archaeological evidence. There are even a few exposed lengths of stone surface on the Pennines and North York Moors. Ordnance Survey maps show the courses of these main roads but in between these must have been a network of lesser tracks linking villas, hamlets and farmsteads.

SUMMARY

So this was the history of our landscape within which our fledgling villages were to form. A manmade countryside, well farmed to the point of exhaustion in places, and showing the scars of previous peoples and empires. Out of the still Dark Ages people in some areas, and for reasons unknown, started to settle in larger groups, to change the way they farmed and to work together as a community rather than family unit. The next chapter describes the formation and relatively short heyday of our English villages.

STILL THERE
FEATURES TO LOOK OUT FOR

■ *FIG 1.14: SEVEN BARROWS, BERKSHIRE: Two of the seven barrows in this field can be seen here, one in front of the tree and the other behind it to the right. These Bronze Age round barrows can be found in areas all over the country but usually they remain as marks in fields which can only be seen from aerial photographs or are marked on maps.*

■ *FIG 1.15: UFFINGTON HILLFORT, OXON: A view from the ramparts of an Iron Age hillfort with its interior to the left and the deep ditch to keep invaders out running down to the right. Originally there would have been a timber palisade running along the top of the bank.*

■ *FIG 1.16: CHEDWORTH ROMAN VILLA (NT) GLOS: A section of tessellated (mosaic) floor with the hypocaust (space for underfloor heating) exposed in the top right corner. Although only in exceptional circumstances are remains like these discovered, villa buildings are common in lowland England often showing up as crop marks on aerial photographs.*

■ *FIG 1.17: DEVIL'S DITCH, CAMBS: This huge bank and ditch cutting straight across the countryside was part of a series of defences which probably date from the late Roman or Saxon period. There are numerous ditches and dykes all across the countryside, some dating as far back as the Iron Age, most of which are believed to have marked the boundary of territories and kingdoms.*

■ *FIG 1.18: BRIXWORTH CHURCH, NORTHAMPTONSHIRE:*
The arch above this later doorway is composed of thin Roman bricks which the Saxon builders of this minster church reused from nearby remains.

■ *FIG 1.19: COVEHITHE, SUFFOLK:*
*This dramatic end to the road shows how coastal erosion is even today
threatening villages. Five miles down the coast from here is the village of
Dunwich, a busy centre in the medieval period which is now mostly under
the sea!*

CHAPTER 2
ESTABLISHMENT AND EXPANSION

ANGLO SAXON AND EARLY MIDDLE AGES: AD 700 to 1300

■ *FIG 2.1: We have moved on 1,200 years from the view in Chapter 1 and our imaginary village is now taking shape. In the middle distance stands the simple stone and thatch church built by the local lord who lives in the timber manor house to the left of it. A new extension of the village is being laid out with rectangular plots for the peasants, each with a humble dwelling and its own croft for growing root crops. This overlooks a green area on which cattle and sheep are currently grazing, but which once a week supports a market, the right to hold it having just been granted to the lord of the manor who is looking for a profitable return for all this investment.*

To the right of the church is the majority of the village which is sprawled along the road down to the river crossing and local water mill. Beyond this is the mound of a motte and bailey castle, which is falling into disuse since it was last used in the civil war some fifty years before while, on the woodclad hill to its left, a new church stands within the old Iron Age hillfort.

Our village has replaced the scattering of farmsteads which made up the picture in the previous period. This chapter will look at the reasons why this change occurred, the physical appearance of these new settlements and what elements of them you may be able to recognise in your village today.

THE NATIONAL PICTURE

As England started to emerge from the Dark Ages (so named due to lack of documentary history rather than being a period which people at the time would have recognised) we find the large kingdoms of firstly Northumbria, then Mercia and finally Wessex vying with each other for supremacy. By the middle of the 9th century the country comprised many distinct ethnic groups, the most prominent being the Angles, Saxons and the British. The latter, so-called Celtic peoples, were the remnants of the native population of Roman Britain. The degree to which they were forced into the west and north by the incoming Germanic tribes or integrated with them is currently a hotly debated issue.

It was at this time that the quarrelling kingdoms faced a new external threat from Vikings (a general historic term probably from the Scandinavian word to wander, which is applied to people from Denmark, Norway and Sweden). They defeated all but the men of Wessex, who under King Alfred the Great halted their progress and split the country in two with his kingdom to the south and west, and 'Danelaw' to the north and east. Alfred was notably one of the first leaders to proclaim himself King of the English, and he and his successors over the next fifty years returned the country to Anglo Saxon control.

Most of the Wessex gains were lost under King Ethelred the Unready and during the first half of the 11th century England was alternately under Danish or Anglo Saxon rule, until finally in 1066 the invading Normans, themselves of Viking origin, took control. To pay back his loyal supporters William the Conqueror granted the estates of the Anglo Saxons to his barons, who in turn built motte and bailey castles on their new manors as powerful symbols designed to quell any thoughts of rebellion. When the natives did rise as they did three times in the Northumbrian territory, William wreaked terrifying revenge by systematically destroying their villages in an act known as the 'Harrying of the North'. The Conqueror's lasting testimony though is the Domesday Book which he commissioned to record the value of manors (not actual villages) so he could calculate how much tax to charge. This instilled such fear in the mainly Anglo Saxon population that they compared it to the Last Judgement, hence the name Domesday.

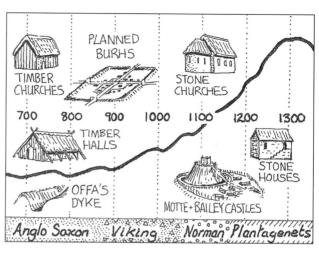

■ *FIG: 2.2: The line shows the population recovering from the lows of the Dark Ages up to a peak of around 5-6 million in the late 13th century.*

William's sons left England with a problem of succession. From 1136 to 1154 King Stephen and the Empress Matilda fought for the throne in a civil war which saw the collapse of central power and the building of numerous 'illegal' castles by local barons who increased their privileges and power amid the anarchy. Despite further disputes between the Crown and its lords, the 12th and 13th centuries were a boom time which saw an increasing population peak at 5-6 million. This was only possible because of an increased output in farming.

ORGANISING OF THE LANDSCAPE

Great changes occurred in the ownership and layout of agricultural land in this period, the reasons for and details of which are still not clear today. The appearance of villages replacing scattered farmsteads and hamlets seems inexorably tied in with this reorganisation.

Around the beginning of this period most of the country was divided into large estates, some owned by the various kings, others having been granted to the new monasteries. At the centre of these estates was the 'caput', which might be a hall or palace, perhaps with an associated hamlet or village, where produce and manpower were collected from the subsidiary settlements around it. The land was divided up into 'infields' close to the settlements, for the growing of crops, and 'outfields' further away, for grazing and resources. Caputs were sometimes established on old Roman villas or within disused Iron Age hillforts, demonstrating continuity if not consistent use.

Within these estates there would have been all the agricultural and natural resources required by the local lord, which has led them to be called 'multiple' estates. Although there are regional variations and names this type of territory has been recognised at various sites all over the country. It is also worth noting that the name of the caput was usually the same as that of the whole estate, and they could be among the earliest of place names, often referring to a natural feature like a river. Therefore if you find your village name in early records it may actually be referring to an estate or caput from which your later settlement may be descended. Some Saxon land charters also survive which can give detailed accounts on the boundary of these and later estates.

The Viking incursions and later permanent settlement of the 9th century led to the break up of large numbers of these estates. In order to buy loyalty or to repay service Anglo Saxon kings and the Viking leaders granted parts of their estates to faithful subjects, so by 1066 some English lords had gained great holdings of land. The arrival of the Normans though led to a virtually complete reorganisation as William the Conqueror granted these estates to his victorious barons, with their allocation not usually matching that of the previous English lord. These new 'baronies' were composed of individual 'manors' or 'vills' while castles and monasteries often replaced old caputs as estate centres. One element of the Saxon past which did survive was the 'hundreds', subdivisions of the counties, the boundaries of which may relate to some of the earlier large estates.

Open Field System

Alongside these changes in ownership was a gradual conversion from an enclosed network of fields farmed mainly by family units, to an open field system worked by a community. This change was not universal, large areas especially in upland England but also in parts of Essex, Kent and especially Devon were never affected. It was also a gradual process which was still developing long after the Norman Conquest, and although we know it was not introduced by the first Saxon settlers, its true origins are still illusive.

The important element of this so-called open field system was co-operation within the new community centred on the village. The old fields would have been opened up into usually two or three great fields, each of which would have been subdivided into 'furlongs'. These in turn were broken down into individual holdings of land or 'strips' which were tenanted by a peasant farmer who would hold a number of them scattered around the fields. Such was the organisation though that his neighbour in the field might well be his neighbour back in the village! The community as a whole would meet and decide the crops to be grown in which field and when. Although it may have been the norm to grow the

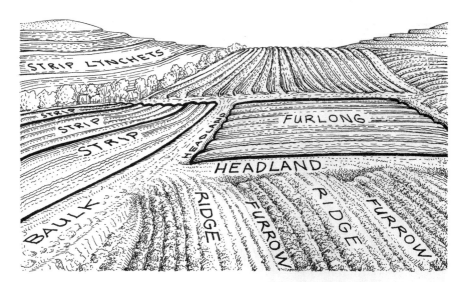

■ FIG: 2.3: A view of an open field showing the various sub-divisions. On the hillsides horizontal steps called lynchets have been formed where the slope was too steep. The remains of these lynchets, headlands, ridges and furrows can be found around many villages today.

same crop across the whole field, there are cases where individual strips may have been planted differently or left fallow for grazing. It was important that grazing of livestock on the fields left fallow, the wastelands and the meadows was also strictly controlled. As these great fields were open there were no boundaries between the individual strips, so disputes between farmers were a regular feature of the Manor Courts and often occur in old court rolls.

This method of farming in common did occur in the other areas of England but it fitted within the existing fields which may have been just subdivided into a few strips. Another element of this system was the lord's own land, the demesne, on which crops and livestock were grown for his and his entourage's consumption. This links into the feudal system which is explained further on. The above description is only a generalisation, as there were inevitably regional variations determined by who owned the land and its geology.

There were also further complications of this simple two or three field system especially, due firstly to the rules governing inheritance of a peasant's holding. In some places it was passed on to the eldest son so there should have been little change to the holding, but in others it was split between the sons leading to ever more complex and fluctuating divisions. Secondly, as the population grew, more land was required to go under the plough, and new fields were cut into the surrounding wastes and woodland. This process, called 'assarting', could have been done by a group who would split the new field equally or by an individual, whose name may still be used for this land. In many cases though these extensions were later incorporated into the common field system, hence complicating the original arrangement.

The importance of the open field system if it existed around your village is the role it played in its formation. It may have been the growth of a hamlet into a village which necessitated the change of field system, or the decision to farm in an open field system which meant that the hamlets had to form a new village. Whichever way round it will be hard to establish the date without archaeological or documentary evidence, but you can piece together the village which resulted by recognising the elements of this system in the field today.

Ridge and Furrow

The most easily recognisable parts of the open field system which you may be able to see around your village are 'ridges' and 'furrows'. It is important to note that they were not formed to represent the individual strips, but are more a creation of the method required to plough the strip. By this time the plough had developed to include not just a coulter and share to cut the soil but a mouldboard as well which turned it over. When ploughing his long, thin strip, the farmer would start in one direction which would force the soil inwards and then would repeat the process as he returned along the other side. This would over a period of time cause the soil of his strip to build up into a long ridge. This may have been a deliberate policy as some have suggested to aid drainage, although the evidence for this logical theory is not always consistent.

Another feature of ridges and furrows is the gentle curve or reverse S shape they tend to form when looked on from above. This is a result of the difficulty of moving the plough and the team of up to eight oxen onto the strip which had to be done by turning them into it to avoid damaging the neighbour's crop. Access to the strip was from the headland, which often developed into a substantial bank as the soil which fell off the ploughs built up over the centuries. Today, where the ridges and furrows have been destroyed it may still be possible to see the remains of the headlands.

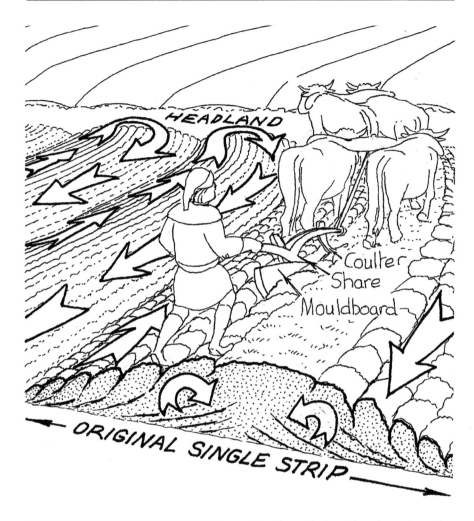

■ *FIG: 2.4: RIDGE AND FURROW: The section through the ridge shows how the action of the mouldboard in turning over the earth, causing the soil to build up in the middle of the strip, formed the ridges and furrows. The arrows on top show the direction of the plough team and how they had to turn onto the headland creating the reversed S shape of the ridges when viewed from above.*

Sheep Clearances

Meanwhile in the upland regions of England other great changes were occurring in the landscape. New monasteries were being founded or refounded and large tracts of land granted to them for financial support. Rents and profits from the produce of these lands paid for such grand stone buildings as Fountains Abbey.

During the 12th and 13th centuries though, these monasteries discovered there was more profit to be made from sheep. English wool was highly valued on the continent, and entrepreneurial monks seem to have discarded Christian morals for a new business doctrine. They cleared their lands and in some cases whole villages, replacing them with granges (a monastic farm) from which the great flocks of sheep were managed. Although the previous grazing of sheep did not leave the visible traces on today's landscape that the ridge and furrow did, the actions of the monks can be seen in the establishment of some of our present-day villages in this period of clearances.

Woodland

This was another important part of the medieval village landscape. Whether it be in an open field system or upland pastoral area, no house could be built or fence erected unless there was a good source of timber. The impression though of dark, forbidding forests where the simple peasant would fear to tread is false. Every part of the woodland was managed, so the cropping and felling of trees would have made the medieval wood a light and, with the flowers that would have grown in the gaps, a colourful place!

Some trees like oak and elm would have been allowed to fully grow so their timber could be used for the major constructional parts of buildings. Other trees like hazel would have been coppiced, that is cut back to the stump every 5-20 years to encourage thin, straight branches to grow, which were used for fencing or to make the wicker type panels (wattle) in between the timbers of the houses. Hedges were also a major source of timber where a tree could grow larger than within a wood as there was no restriction of space.

The right to cut and collect wood was shared between peasants and parishes and was as tightly managed as the strips in the fields! To protect woodland from grazing animals a bank would have been raised around its perimeter with a ditch on the outside face. These can still be found sometimes surprisingly within a wood showing that the area of trees has increased since medieval times!

Another source of wood was wood pasture, which was usually common land with trees and open spaces for grazing. To avoid the livestock eating the young shoots of the trees, they were pollarded, whereby the tree is cut back above the reach of the grazing animals. Pollarded willows were a common site along the riverbank, with the cropped branches (osiers) used for basket weaving. It is worth noting that a coppiced or pollarded tree will often be up to two or three times older than an unmanaged tree of the same species, although willows are rarely very old. This also applies to those trees which were cut back and laid to make traditional hedges. Identification of these around your village may help in establishing old from new boundaries and previous land use.

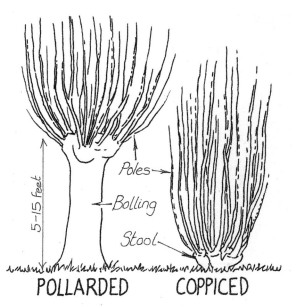

■ *FIG 2.5: Diagram showing pollarded and coppiced trees. Both can still be found in the countryside today though usually with larger poles due to neglect in cutting.*

Forest Law

The favourite pastime of many a medieval king was the now contentious subject of hunting. To protect the woodlands and the deer and wild boars which they hunted, the Normans introduced Forest Law.

This forbade poaching and prevented agricultural expansion into the protected area but allowed deer to graze on the surrounding crops and huntsmen to trample over the fields in pursuit of their prey, much to the annoyance of the local lord and peasant alike. The fines imposed for offences were a useful source of revenue for the Crown, so during the 12th century the area of land under Forest Law was expanded and by 1200 more than a fifth of England was affected.

It is important to note though that the area under Forest Law was not all woodland. For instance the relatively treeless Dartmoor and Exmoor were covered, while the whole of the reasonably well-farmed county of Essex was at one point under the influence of Forest Courts. In fact only about a quarter of the land under Forest Law was actually wooded!

The resentment felt towards this royal imposition may have been one of the reasons for the emergence of the Robin Hood legends in the 13th century. By then though it was becoming financially beneficial to the king to charge a lord for permission to extend his fields into the wooded areas (assarting) and to lose the income from the fines. Gradually the area under Forest Law was reduced although it was not completely abolished until 1660.

Deer Parks

The passion for hunting was shared by the lesser nobility and any self respecting lord would have to, or aspire to, own a deer park. Typically this would be established within an existing wood on the lord's own demesne land, around which was constructed a bank with a hedge or paling (a fence made from vertical pointed timbers) on top, and within this a ditch to prevent the precious animals escaping. The deer would then be released out into the surrounding land at the

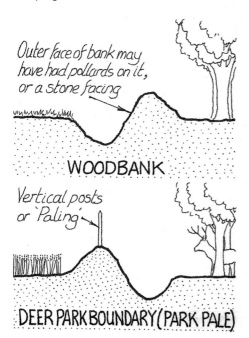

FIG 2.6: Sections through a woodbank with the ditch on the outside to keep livestock in the field, and a deer park boundary with an inner ditch to keep the valuable animals within the wood.

time of a hunt. At their peak there were some 3,000 parks across England which could be up to 200 acres in size. The remains of their internal ditches and external banks (as opposed to the other way round with a woodbank) can still be identified today.

The remainder of the land, be it meadows, heaths, wastes or commons, was used to graze livestock or for its material resources. By the 13th century meadows were the most important areas, usually along the banks of rivers where flooding would enrich the soil. They would have been divided up into 'doles' or 'strips' so peasants would share the crop of hay and then let their animals out to graze. This was becoming more important as the pressure of a rising population, which desperately needed more land under the plough, meant that the increasing numbers of animals to pull them needed larger quantities of feed. This boom time in farming even forced peasants to farm upland areas like Dartmoor and the Pennines which had not seen the plough since the Bronze Age and never have since.

THE VILLAGE

For generations we have been taught that this is the period when most of our villages were founded. Work by archaeologists and historians over the past fifty years has not changed this broad date but it has shown how surprisingly complex their establishment and expansion was. We should remove from our minds images of Anglo Saxon invaders surveying a deserted landscape, choosing at will a geographically suitable site and then naming their new village after themselves. As the previous chapter explained the newcomers were fitting into an existing structure of estates and fields, their first settlements were scattered affairs and until at least the 8th century farmsteads and hamlets were the norm.

So when was your village founded? In the form which we are familiar with they appear to have mainly taken shape quite late on, from the 10th-13th centuries. But, some of you may cry, my village has a church with elements dating back to the 8th and 9th centuries, or perhaps an Anglo Saxon charter which mentions its name earlier than this! These factors all prove that there was settlement in the area at that time but not that it was in the form of the village you know today. Take for example our imaginary village in the picture on page 21. The church to the left of centre was built by a Saxon thegn (a lesser nobleman) next to his hall from which he managed his surrounding estate made up of isolated farmsteads. The name and boundary of his estate is recorded by charter and again later in the Domesday Book. But sometime between then and 1200 when the picture is set a new village has been laid out, a process which is continuing in this view.

■ *FIG 2.7: The left hand cartoon shows the traditional image of the founding of villages by our Saxon ancestors, while the right hand version is probably nearer the truth.*

It has taken the name of the old estate, the boundary of which has also been reused to mark the limits of the new parish. This is a simple example of what you may find in your village to be a more elaborate set of events.

Two points to remember when looking at this period of your village's history is the huge time scale involved, some six hundred years, and that our predecessors would have had the same desires, aspirations and abilities to change their surroundings as we do. In many village histories a statement is made of the foundation, then the following thousand years are covered by the phrase 'nothing much happened' or 'life went on as usual' until suddenly in the well-documented last few centuries the village mysteriously springs into life. This gives the reader the false impression that in the period of this chapter the lord and peasant alike were uninterested in bettering their situation or unable to do so. Now in the light of modern discoveries and thinking you may be able to fill in these gaps in the history of your village.

SETTLEMENT TYPES

Although the reasons for a village's establishment and development are varied, there are some recognisable patterns which when you peel off the past five hundred years of building you may be able to identify. Firstly there is the question of how the village formed.

It may be surprising to find out that many of the villages in England are believed to have been at some stage fully or at least partly planned! In most examples that have been studied the tell-tale signs of straight and rectangular road and boundary patterns have been identified and it has been the later encroachment, and the break up of these divisions, that has blurred the original regular layout.

In the first case there were existing settlements which were extended or relaid out in this period. In a medieval village encircled by its own fields, with any wasteland used for grazing, and a lord overseeing it all, the peasants were limited in where they could put another house as the population grew. Any extension to the village or a replanning of it would have to be agreed to or initiated by the lord of the manor and then divided out, most likely into equal sized plots. With only simple surveying techniques available these would have to be regular and rectilinear, more like Milton Keynes than Milton under Wychwood!

In other cases villages would have been planned from scratch especially where land was being reclaimed. The Fens of East Anglia and other marshy areas were drained and new settlements established, while in areas like Yorkshire, devastated by William the Conqueror's 'Harrying of the North' or by raids from the Scots, new villages were laid out on the wasteland. It also seems that the reason behind a lot of this planning was a commercial one by the respective lords of the manor, in particular ones owned by the Church! If they owned a plot of relatively useless land from which they could only expect low rents, it surely made more sense to put people on it who could farm the former wastes and dramatically increase their revenue.

Another common financial venture was to try and establish a market in the village. This would cost the lord of the manor initially as he had to pay for a Royal Grant and then lay out a green area for the market with probably housing around it. The potential profits to be gained from rents for the stalls and plots though was enough to outweigh this, and it became especially popular in the late 12th and 13th centuries. Many of these ventures failed and the village never grew, while the successful ones developed into towns.

Some villages must have been unplanned and expanded haphazardly, perhaps because the development was illegal or the lord of the manor let it grow in an unregulated manner. These could be linear settlements which grew along a road, a sprinkling of house plots based around an early industry like iron working, quarrying or potteries, or a village on land newly claimed from woods or marshes. It will perhaps be found that the majority of villages grew with both the above planned and unplanned elements.

TYPES OF PLANS

It is difficult to characterise all the possible layouts for planned villages but there are a few common patterns shown here in Fig 2.8 in their medieval form, which you may be able to recognise in villages today. In the plans it is worth noting how the crosses which mark the church and original focus of the village are even at this early date being sidelined. The shift of the village to new centres, in these cases around the greens, demonstrates how the layout of a village is not fixed in the landscape but moves to meet new social or economic demands.

THE VILLAGE ELEMENTS
Church and Parish

The arrival of the Vikings in the 9th century not only involved the robbing of the minsters and monasteries but also, as previously mentioned, led to the breaking up the old large multiple estates into smaller holdings. These two factors seem to have weakened the power of the minsters, and during the following centuries a new network of smaller churches and parishes appeared.

Outdoing his neighbour was just as important to the ambitious Saxon landowner as it can be to some today. They had come into possession of these new small estates and desired the latest in status symbols by which promotion to the rank of 'thegn' could be achieved. The answer in order to ascend the secular social ladder was to build a church. The fact that his estate workers had a roof over their head and did not have as far to walk in order to pray was probably a minor consideration.

The new churches were usually sited next to the thegn's manor house. Most of them would have been of timber construction with a nave and chancel and a thatched roof above, similar in design to Fig 1.10 (see page 19). There were some of stone, perhaps on wealthier or royal estates, while the old minster churches (which were often sited next to royal palaces anyway) still played a role in the new ecclesiastical structure.

The lord of the manor though would have had no intention of paying for the upkeep of his new church, in fact one of the reasons for building it was that the thegn could make a profit from his investment! The church would have had an endowment of land when founded, its 'glebe', the income from which was intended to support the priest. The villagers also had to pay to bury someone in the churchyard, while the lord of the manor would be able to appoint a priest of his choice to look after his flock. Although the old minster churches would try and hang on to these valuable rights, the lord of the manor would endeavour to have them transferred to his new church.

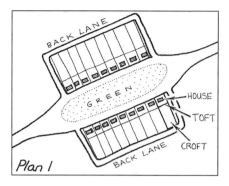

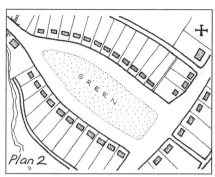

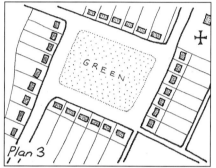

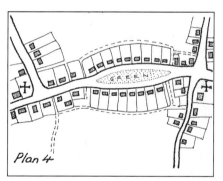

■ FIG 2.8: Plans 1-3 show possible layouts on a straight, T shaped and grid plan with regular plots laid out to set sizes. The green was not an essential ingredient in these plans and where it did exist it has often been built on or broken up at a later date.

Plan 4 on the other hand shows a situation where two separate hamlets have been made into one village by the laying out of a green area between them. This 'polyfocal' type of layout takes many forms sometimes involving many separate hamlets.

Plan 5 is an imaginary village which has had the elements of plans 1-3 added on at different times, so although it looks unorganised, the majority of it was planned. With all these layouts it is the later breaking up, selling off or abandonment of the regular plots which gives the impression that they developed naturally.

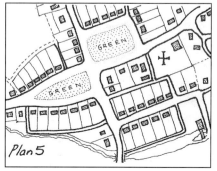

More important still was in the 10th century when the Saxon kings wrote the payment tithes, a contribution of 10% of the villagers' produce for the upkeep of the church, into law. To determine which church you paid this to, parish boundaries were established, and as most of the new churches were serving an estate it was logical that the parish boundary would follow the estate boundary. This means that although there have been subsequent changes to parishes, especially in the 19th century, these boundaries can record old estates which have long since vanished. The parish in this context is an ecclesiastical area; the secular equivalent was usually in the north called a 'township' or a 'vill', while in the south it could also be known as a 'tithing'. A township, vill or tithing could follow the same boundary as the parish, while in others there may have been a number of them within one parish. The study of these is a valuable tool in tracing the history of your village and it is worth reading further about them before trying to evaluate the information.

When the Normans arrived they found and recorded in the Domesday Book an ecclesiastical system still in a state of change from the old minster system, which continued to have some influence especially in the west and north, to one dominated by the parish church. Although there were many local complications, towards the end of the 12th century the process was virtually complete. By now though the local lords were losing interest in their churches as a profit making enterprise. Across Europe a return to the real meaning of the faith and the influence of the Pope was directing the incomes and rights of the Church into the hands of the clergy. This was a time of piety, Crusades and pilgrims. New monasteries were established and the wealthy would endow them with land and the upkeep of and hence profits from their churches. By 1300 the control of the parish was firmly in the hands of the bishops and monasteries.

Another benefit of this upsurge in Christian faith along with the arrival of the now wealthy Normans was the rebuilding of the churches, especially in stone. The new churches were larger, often with a central tower, and had Romanesque arches supported by thick, round columns and decorated with chevrons. The introduction in the late 12th century of the pointed (Gothic) arch permitted a lighter structure with finer columns and the appearance of basic tracery in the windows. By the end of this period a church more familiar to our eyes was appearing with a west tower, followed by a nave and chancel, yet the exterior and interior decoration and details would have shocked us!

The outside would most likely have been plastered over and painted, perhaps with a limewash. The rough stone walls underneath were never intended to be revealed, it was only during Victorian restoration that they were stripped and

■ FIG 2.9: An imaginary Norman village scene with a new stone church. Note the thatched roof, small deep set windows and whitewashed walls.

exposed. The statues and patterns on the west front and doorways may have been lavishly painted but these were mostly destroyed in the 16th and 17th centuries. Inside a riot of colour would have greeted you, once your eyes had adjusted to the gloom. Paintings of scenes from the Bible adorned the walls while bright colours highlighted the patterns around the arches, but again these were usually whitewashed over by later zealous Anglicans. There would have been no pews and only rarely stained glass; the window openings would have been covered by drapes of animal skin or a sacking. We are used to locking our churches to protect them from burglary, in the Middle Ages it was the stone font which was secured - so that its holy water could not be used in witchcraft! As we were a Catholic country at this time there was no pulpit, the various ceremonies and mass being conducted at the altar and in Latin. The illiterate masses listening in the nave would not have understood a word that was spoken, but the pictures on the walls left them in no doubt what would happen to them if they strayed from the Faith.

Those who had passed on to the other side would have been buried in the churchyard, though as you can see in Fig 2.9 this would have looked bare

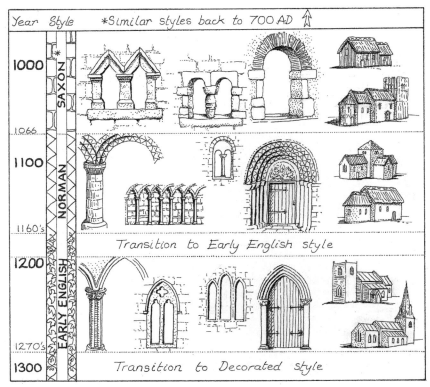

■ FIG 2.10: A chart showing some of the features and styles of churches and the architectural style and date to which they belong.

compared to today's medley of gravestones. There would have been just a single cross to cover the whole area with only the important few being fortunate enough to be buried in the church. If you could not make it within then you might at least try and get as close to the altar as you could on the outside. Most peasants would have been wrapped in cloth and buried in an east-west direction, while the better off might have a stone-lined cist grave or even a stone coffin. Within the church the tombs from the 12th century were most commonly covered by a single slab set in the floor with a shallow carving of the occupant adorning it. In the following century these developed into carvings in relief then into more familiar raised rectangular tombs richly adorned by the stone mason.

Although we assume that the simple village folk were humbled in the sight of God, they were actually remarkably disrespectful. The church could be used for social events, with market stalls being set up where the pews now stand, while financial deals could be sealed in the porch and heated discussions take place in the church grounds. Our view of hard and grey churches is very much an Anglican creation, the role and appearance in the Middle Ages was much more colourful, mysterious and flexible. Don't be put off by their current hard exterior, the church is usually the most fascinating building in your village and every detail of it down to its very position is valuable in understanding your village's history.

Monasteries and Knights Templars

The influence upon the village of the refounded monasteries was not only in their role as landlord of an increasing number of parish churches and as previously mentioned in clearances for sheep farming but also directly in the removal of whole settlements! The main culprits were the Cistercian monks whose order required them to live in remote places. As we have already discovered the countryside was well populated so when these monks started to build on a new site they had to remove any inconveniently placed villages!

Another influential group in the 12th and 13th century were the Knights Templars (named after the 'Temple' of Solomon in Jerusalem). The success of the First Crusade in 1099, led to a succession of nobles heading off to fight the Pope's chosen enemies. To protect them the Knights Templars were formed, in effect fighting monks, whose order was based along Cistercian principles, and like them they were granted land to support their cause. They managed these estates from preceptories which were built with a keep and usually a circular church within a defensive ditch. Their mounting wealth led to their downfall and dissolution in 1312, with the order's land being passed over to the Knights Hospitallers, although Edward II and others tried to grab as much as they could for themselves.

You may find that your village was directly influenced by the presence of a local monastery or preceptory, or that the monks were its landlords. Look out for village or farm names which contain the word 'Temple' as these often mean that the Knights Templars owned that estate. Also the word Grange which, although it can be just a country house, could date back to an earlier monastic farm.

Tithe Barns

Among the most enduring symbols of the monastic system are their huge tithe barns, some of which date back to the 12th and 13th centuries. All the produce which the monks or other estate owners had rights to, as well as the 10% of all produce which was the villagers' tithe contribution, had to be stored somewhere. Great barns would have been built, most likely in timber but also in stone, and usually aisled with massive upright timbers supporting the great sloping roof.

■ *FIG 2.11: GREAT COXWELL BARN (NT), OXON: This interior view shows the construction method which was required to support the huge expanse of roof with two rows of vertical timbers, in this case resting on the square stone columns, forming the aisles. Saxon and Norman aisled halls would have looked very similar to this, usually smaller in scale, with all timber construction and with solid walls at each end.*

There would have been an opposing set of doors between which the threshing (separating of the grain from the stem of the crop) was performed, this area being known as the 'threshold'. These agricultural cathedrals were usually sited near the manor house or grange and it is a credit to their design and construction that they not only remain standing but also when rediscovered they have often been found still in use.

The Manor House

The estate of the Saxon thegn or Norman lord of the manor would have been managed from a main residence or hall (although not every manor had one). It would have been important not just for the everyday running of the village and fields, but also in a judicial role as the Manor Courts would have been held here.

The earliest residences were great timber halls, not dissimilar to the tithe barns, with rows of timbers forming aisles inside in an otherwise open plan layout. In the middle was an open hearth with the smoke from the fire escaping through a gap in the roof, while in the remainder of the building you would have found the lord and his entourage eating and sleeping communally.

By the 12th and 13th centuries improved timber-framing techniques allowed the walls to be higher and the whole building to have more of the familiar box shape.

■ FIG 2.12: Two 13th century manor houses, the left hand one timber-framed with a central open hall, while the right hand one is stone with the hall on the upper level.

■ FIG 2.13: WEALD AND DOWNLAND OPEN AIR MUSEUM: A reconstruction of a small medieval hall. Typically there is no chimney, the timbers are not painted black and the base of the frame rests on a thin stone foundation.

Although the aisled hall was still popular through the Middle Ages alternative methods using a pair of crucks or posts and trusses (usually called box framing) had the advantage of leaving the interior clear of the obstructions. Further advances at this time included a wooden platform or dais for the lord of the manor, which raised him above the draughty earthen floor, and the first appearance of separate rooms. In an important house the cooking would have been done in a separate building so the hall would not have burnt down if the kitchen caught fire. Stone manor houses start to appear at the end of the 12th century for the wealthiest lords. These were of two storeys with the main hall on the upper floor accessed by external steps, while there was storage below in the undercroft. In the troublesome regions which bordered Wales and Scotland these stone houses, best described as fortified manor houses, could take a more defensive role with only narrow window openings and access to the lower floors sometimes limited to an internal staircase.

Moats

The latest fashion accessory in the 13th century for your new manor house was a moat. Although originally a feature of castles, and still used in a defensive role around fortified manor houses in the border regions, it was rapidly becoming a cosmetic trimming in the less troublesome lowland parts of England. Moats may have been used for water storage or fish ponds but their primary purpose seems to have been to impress the guests. Hundreds of these survive, frequently around farmhouses which themselves can contain architectural remains from as far back as the 13th century, or sometimes just as a continuous ditch forming a rectangular shape in a field. Locating them around your village can help identify the sites of early manor houses and is again essential to piecing together the shape of your village in medieval times.

Fish Ponds

Road and river travel was too basic and slow for sea fish to be transported to all but the coastal areas of England. Freshwater fish were therefore consumed and to keep a reliable supply the lord of the manor would probably have fish ponds created. These would be a set of usually rectilinear pools, linked together and fed by a stream. The earthworks of these fish ponds are still common features and like the moats which they were sometimes linked to can indicate the presence of an important house.

Dovecotes

Another perk of owning a manor was the exclusive right to own pigeons! Not a glamorous privilege these days but in medieval times this food source, along with their eggs, was essential in maintaining a variety to the diet of a lord and his guests through the barren months of winter. Inside these structures were numerous recesses for the birds, and some type of ladder arrangement for their keeper to collect the eggs from.

Castles

The invading Normans had to establish a firm grip on their potentially rebellious Saxon subjects. What better way to keep them in order than to build a huge castle, towering over their timber and mud hovels? In some cases these seem to have been built on the site of a previously fortified Saxon residence, so it could be argued that William the Conqueror brought with him a new style of construction rather than a radically new invention.

The most distinctive early type was a motte and bailey castle where a mound (the motte) was built up in layers and a timber tower (the keep) erected on top. Below the motte to one side a large enclosure (the bailey) was attached within which were the garrison's sleeping quarters, stables and workshops, while the whole site was surrounded by a ditch (the moat, which only contained water if the ground was suitable). The remains of mottes can be found all over England, ranging from as little as 10 ft to 100 ft high, and usually with associated

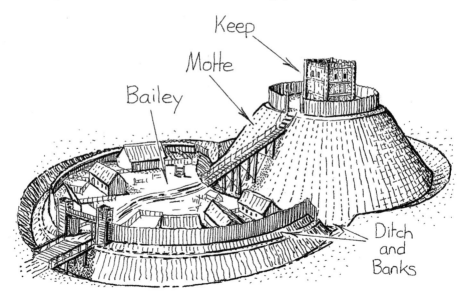

■ FIG 2.14: An early motte and bailey castle as it would have appeared in its original form.

earthworks marking the bailey, but be careful as the raised earthen base of old windmills (mill mounds) or large round barrows can easily be mistaken for them.

Another early type is known as a 'ringwork', where a circular ditch and palisade enclosed a level platform on which the keep and its ancillary buildings stood. These castles may have also reused an old fortification, like a hillfort or Saxon burh, or made use of a natural feature in part of the construction.

The other threat to William's grip on his new conquest came from his very own barons. To ensure they did not become too powerful, the barons had to apply for a royal licence in order to build their own castles. This system collapsed in the civil war of 1136-1154 and led to another spate of building, this time by the local barons who were free to erect their own makeshift castles although these were often pulled down when order was restored under Henry II.

During the 12th and 13th century those castles which did survive were greatly improved. Stone keeps replaced the earlier timber ones, although the motte may have been reduced in height or made obsolete due to the increased weight of the new buildings. Larger or extra baileys may have been added with surrounding stone walls and heavily guarded gateway arrangements called a barbican. Castles from the late 12th century onwards often had round towers to reduce the threat of collapse, which could be caused by your enemy tunnelling under the corner of a square keep, and also to help deflect the impact of missiles from the latest siege machines.

These successful castles are mainly a feature of towns; you are more likely to find the remains of a short-lived motte and bailey or ringwork castle around your village today. If it is located near a river crossing, at the head of a valley or some other important military position then it may date back to the Conquest; if the position seems less strategic then it may have been erected by your local baron between 1136 and 1154.

Peasants' Houses

Although the lord of the manor would have lived in some luxury, the remaining villagers were housed in far less glamorous buildings. These were not the quaint timber-framed two-storeyed cottages which are a vital component of our quintessential English village today. In the medieval period they were usually a single storey 'long house', with just one room in which the villager not only worked, ate and slept but also kept his livestock! As they would only last for around 20 to 30 years they were not built with substantial foundations if any at all, so you are unlikely to find any remains of them other than the platform on which they stood.

YE OLDE D.I.Y. SHOPPE
An easy to follow guide to building your own
CRUCK FRAMED COTTAGE

1

Alternatively it can be split by pegs

Axe
a.
b. Saw
Pit
c.

a. Square off your main curving timber.
b. Cut it in two over a saw pit.
c. You will then have two symmetrical CRUCKS.

2

Mortice + Tenon

frame can be un-assembled for transporting to site.

Now assemble frames of cottage using mainly mortice and tenon joints. Number the joints so they can be reassembled on site.

3

'The Rearing'

Cill

a bay

Once reassembled, the frames can be lifted into position and timbers fitted between them to form the BAYS.

4

Wattle
Window
daub

Infill the timber frame with WATTLE (a weave of oak or hazel pieces) and apply DAUB to inner + outer surfaces. Paint when dry.

■ FIG 2.15: A imaginary instruction guide to build a medieval peasant's house.

No peasant could afford to buy masonry, and bricks had not been reintroduced at this time, so he would have used locally available materials from which to build his home. By the 12th and 13th centuries the wooden huts of the early Saxon settlers had developed into timber-framed buildings which at this time were most likely to have been of a crucks type in which a curving tree was cut in two to make matching supports. Once this frame had been erected the gaps were filled in with a weave of oak staves or hazel branches and then coated inside and out with a daub, made of a mixture of mud, clay, straw, animal hair and cow dung! These exterior panels were painted with a limewash, although colour could be added with for instance bulls' blood to make a pink, while the oak timbers were usually left unfinished. The familiar black paint on the frame was a Victorian idea, the cottage exterior up until then would have been refreshingly light, with white panels framed in greying oak and with a fresh splash of golden straw covering the roof (similar to the house in Fig 2.13).

In other parts of the country the walls could have been made from local stones, although timber was still required for the roof trusses. In other areas, most notably the South West, they might have used cob which is made from blocks of mud and straw built up in layers, producing thick, slightly sloping walls with rounded corners. Thatch was almost exclusively the roofing material and usually made from straw which the peasant would have as a by product of his arable crop. Reeds lasted better but were harder to find and unnecessary as the buildings didn't stand long anyway. Turf and flat stone slabs may also have been used especially in the poorer or upland areas. All the above methods were still in use until the transport revolution of the 19th century made bricks, slates and tiles readily available and cheap.

■ *FIG 2.16: The open interior of a peasant's longhouse with the livestock at the far end.*

The Mill

The other important building you were likely to find in your medieval village was the mill and within it the much loathed miller. They had a monopoly on grinding the peasants' grain and were renowned for excessive charging. Another bad habit was blocking the river or stream to boat traffic so they could build up a good head of water to turn their wheel. These mills were always powered by water wheels and although the remains of the later buildings may have gone, the header pond, weirs and channels can sometimes still be found.

The windmill only appears in the 13th century and was probably introduced into this country by Crusader knights who had seen them on the continent. They would have solved the problem of grinding grain when your village had no suitable water supply. These early ones would have been simple post mills whereby the sails and upper parts are supported on a vertical post so that they could be turned to face the wind. No mill this old still stands today but the mound on which they were erected may still exist.

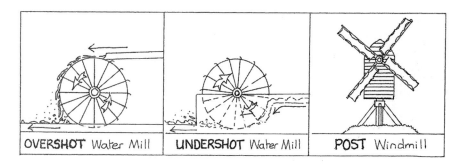

■ *FIG 2.17: Diagrams showing the different types of mills in this period.*

The Green

Greens to our modern minds are an essential ingredient of the English village. These apparently ancient strips of common land are arenas for all its communal activities and evoke great passions when its bounds are threatened. Yet the green today may only have been laid out in the 19th century for its ascetic value and numerous older ones have been built upon in later times when it was not seen as a vital part of the village. If it is ancient then it probably took shape in this period.

The origins of a village green can be impossible to establish except in the cases where it was part of a planned extension perhaps for a market or part of a completely new village. In other cases the village may have expanded to surround an existing piece of common land, often given the name 'End' or 'Green', although the original village may have later contracted to leave just this isolated cluster of houses around it.

The green had many uses including pasture of livestock, sports on special occasions and a weekly market. These markets were where peasants could purchase everyday commodities like items of hardware, produce they could not grow themselves and salt, which was essential for preserving meat especially over winter. The annual fair was probably the only time they saw more exotic goods though these events were often held outside the village.

Our ideal green is not complete without its pond. These were vital sources of water for livestock and may have been the reason for the establishment of the settlement or they could have been dug on purpose. Other sources of water included wells which at this date were mainly exclusive to castles, manor houses and monastic establishments. The local river, stream or, better still, spring would have been used and even rainwater off roofs was collected in villages even well into the 20th century.

TRANSPORT
Roads

The reasons for travelling to and from your medieval village for the average peasant would have been limited to working the land within the manor and going to market. He was unlikely to own a horse and not everyone had a cart. It was probably not a bad thing that he did not have far to travel as roads during the Middle Ages were on the whole pretty basic and often impassable at the worst times of the year.

There was no Medieval Highways Department so generally the lord of the manor was responsible for the upkeep of the main roads, but it is likely that only the worst of the ruts and pot-holes were ever repaired. Roads were rarely built completely from new except in cases of a planned village or a realignment due to a change in river crossing or to by-pass the lord's new house. Most developed to meet the changing flow of traffic as destinations fluctuated in importance. The local roads which took the peasant to a neighbouring village or market were usually just individual tracks between the fields linked together often with kinks where they met on the parish boundary. In some cases the village may have formed or been laid out at an existing crossroads or along an important road. There was some travel on a national level not only by royalty, bishops, knights and lords moving from one estate or court to another, but also by traders especially in commodities like salt from places like Droitwich and wool from the monastic farms which was destined for Europe. It may be surprising to learn that during the Saxon and medieval period, the well-built main Roman roads were only rarely reused. This is mainly due to the fact that they were part of a national system leading from one town to another. In this period most of those towns had been abandoned and the military and market forces which necessitated the roads had disappeared. The bulk of the population now travelled locally and these engineering marvels simply did not go where they needed to.

The countryside would also have been criss-crossed by numerous tracks and paths taking the villagers and their livestock out into their fields or pasture, while other routes led to natural resources like woodland, quarries or grazing on uplands or waste ground. In exceptional cases some of these may have been used since pre-Roman times especially in the hills and mountains where the geology and an unchanging method of farming limited the choice of routes from the settlements to their fields.

Identifying these ancient routes is an essential part of understanding the history of your village and will help not only in establishing the position and shape of the settlement but also its social and economic relationship with surrounding villages and towns. On the ground older roads and tracks may be recognised by lengths which pass through holloways. This is a cutting formed by the constant use of the route, natural erosion and by farmers who in the past scraped off the dung and mud from the surface of the road to manure their fields. The other features to look for are old hedges and banks lining the sides of the road. These can often be recognised by thick tree trunks, the branches from which have been laid flat to form the hedge, other generally old trees, or by the build up of a bank from generations of growth. In some cases by counting the number of species of flora within a hedge you can approximately date the feature (roughly 1 species equals 30 years of age, e.g. find 10 species and the hedge could be 300 years old). This final method does not seem to work in all regions and can be misleading when dating a hedge which was formed by retaining a belt of existing woodland.

Crossing Rivers

A river or stream was the major obstacle which the road had to cross. The most common method of doing so was the ford. Rivers in this period would have been more open, meandering through flood plains, rather than in tight contained channels as they are today. Fording these shallow waterways was a practical solution although there may have only been a few suitable places along a stretch of river and as a result their location may have attracted settlement long before this period. The problem with a ford is the danger of damaging goods, animals and people in crossing, and the fact that they would have been impassable at times of flooding.

The next step up could have been a low stone or timber structure like a clapper bridge, which appears as no more than a line of stepping stones with slabs or timbers laid across. These simple crossings would only be suitable where the water level would not rise excessively and there was no traffic on the river. Although they are commonly found in the South West and upland regions these bridges usually date to recent centuries and it would be hard to prove any greater antiquity even if the route was medieval.

The most common method of crossing a larger river was by ferry. This could either be simply a man and a rowing boat or more often a flat bottomed vessel would have been dragged across by a rope or chain fixed to both banks. Even where a bridge was built a ferry might continue and in some cases even later replace the permanent structure when it decayed. This could happen when the lord of the manor who had the right to charge for use of the ferry found this more profitable than having to spend on the expensive construction or repair of a bridge.

Where bridges were built they probably started in timber, and using similar methods to the Romans. Stone piers or wooden piles were erected across the river and then timber planks laid across. Stone bridges started to appear in the 12th and 13th centuries but mainly in towns and cities. A line of small pointed arches with thick piers between them and an angled cutwater providing a refuge for pedestrians was the most typical style of the day. They would usually have been narrow with just enough room for a cart to cross and may not have had a parapet, with just a timber barrier or nothing at all to protect the person crossing from the water below.

River Travel

River and coastal travel was the other method of moving around, especially large cargoes like masonry or timber. The medieval boatman though faced just as many hazards and difficulties as there would have been on land. Obstructions across the river like a bridge which may not have been big enough to navigate through, especially when the water was high, and most onerous of all the weirs erected by millers to build up a head of water in order to turn their wheels. Thirteenth century law saw the gradual removal of this latter problem although the boats would still have to pass through treacherous flash locks. These consisted of vertical paddles which were lifted out by hand and their supporting beam swung aside allowing the downstream traffic to be literally flushed through

■ *FIG 2.18: An early timber and later stone bridge. Note that although both are shown with parapets these were often added at a later date.*

the gap, and when the water level each side had evened the upstream traffic could be dragged through. The other main problem was the level of the water itself, which when high in winter made travel downstream hazardous and upstream near impossible, while in summer the low levels led to regular groundings and loss of cargo.

The limitations of this transport system became more of a problem in the centuries to follow as trade and travel on a national level began to increase. In his isolated village community the average medieval peasant was only concerned with moving about in his parish and to the local market.

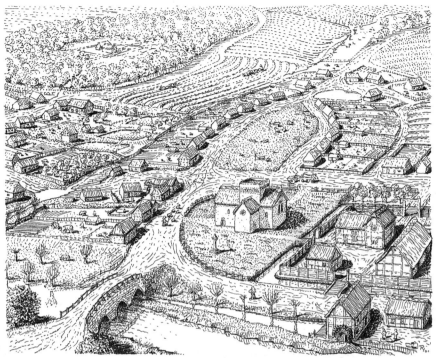

■ *FIG 2.19: A view over an imaginary medieval village containing the elements discussed above from the deer park in the top left corner to the manor house complex and mill in the bottom right.*

THE VILLAGERS

During this later Saxon and early medieval period the people living in the village were to varying degrees influenced by what has become known since the 18th century as the feudal system. The basic principle is that the lord or king gave the tenancy of a piece of land (or fee) to an underling who in return gave him military service when called upon. So if we picked a fight with France the lord of the manor would be required to supply a number of knights and peasants to the national fighting force. Although a convenient arrangement in theory it would appear to have only made up part of the armies, as mercenaries were found to be more effective soldiers than an untrained peasant wielding a fork who may have to return to his fields if the battle clashed with harvest time! Also this military service only seems to have been applied effectively in the 11th and 12th centuries and after the Magna Carta in 1215 it fell from favour, not helped by rebellious barons who would resist supplying arms even to the extent of barricading themselves in their castles.

At a local level the feudal system varied regionally in its structure and in the degrees with which it was applied. In the great swathe of villages across Middle England which were surrounded by their two or three large communal fields it was crucial for the smooth running of the agricultural system. In other areas which maintained the older infield and outfield system like Devon, Essex and upland England, or which were cut out of wastelands in the 12th and 13th centuries as in North Warwickshire, the Fens and parts of the Yorkshire Dales, the feudal system was less influential.

To the peasant (in this description a 'villein') this meant he had to give not only military service, but had to work his lord's own demesne land, give him a quantity of his arable produce and some livestock, perhaps even give him money, and all this on top of his tithe payment to the church. In return he would in theory gain the protection of his lord, the right to appeal to the Manor Court and the security of knowing his place in this strongly hierarchical society. Although the odds seem stacked against the peasant there were ways of softening the blow of his obligations, for instance he might send a less able or lazy member of the family to work the lord's land or give him only his poorest livestock.

It is also misleading to refer to all those who laboured on the land as peasants, for there were many levels of status within this broad band, just as there are in an office or factory today. A freeman would be greatly insulted if he was called a cottar, in the same way as a supervisor in a factory would be if he was referred to as a tea-boy! The categories varied over time and region but by the 12th and 13th century the following groupings were the most prominent. Below the lord of the manor was a freeman or franklin who was as the name suggests someone

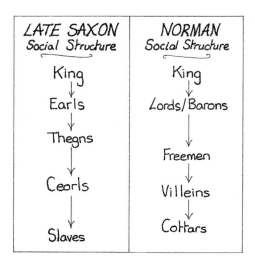

LATE SAXON Social Structure	NORMAN Social Structure
King	King
Earls	Lords/Barons
Thegns	Freemen
Ceorls	Villeins
Slaves	Cottars

■ FIG 2.20:
A simplified list of the Saxon and Norman village social structures.

who was free of obligations of service to the lord. He would still have to do some jobs, perhaps supervise at harvesting or he might be the miller, but in general he paid a rent for his land and could therefore invest money back into his holding. Next down the ladder was the largest group, the villeins, who tenanted scattered strips of land by performing duties which have been previously described. From this band would come specialist workers like the blacksmith, a reeve (who was responsible for collecting rent) and a priest of a poorer parish. At the bottom were cottars who were judged on their small holding of land or worst of all if they tenanted land from one of their neighbours rather than the lord. This group could include those who did the ploughing and herding on the demesne land or looked after the lord's wood and grain.

The village as a community would agree at regular meetings which crops should be grown in which field and at what time. The inevitable disagreements and disputes would be heard at the Manor Court and the records (or court rolls) from these can be an interesting insight into the social workings of your village. The village would also be part of a hundred or wapentake, a subdivision of a shire, which were taking shape in the early 11th century. Each hundred would have its own court where the freemen from the villages would meet to resolve local disputes and matters of law and order. In 1279, Edward I ordered a survey of villages to ascertain who held which land within each hundred. Known as the Hundred Rolls it was more comprehensive than the Domesday Book but unfortunately the returns for only five counties survive.

SUMMARY

Within the restrictions of a book of this size the above description of the components of your village is a brutal generalisation. It will hopefully help to introduce the basic elements of your village's structure in this period, a structure which in some cases lasted through the time frames of the following chapters and up to the 19th century. Other villages were not so fortunate. A lord surveying his manor on the eve of the 14th century may have been looking forward to many more prosperous years and further expansion of his holdings. He would have been unlikely to see the cracks which were already appearing in the rapidly overstretched agricultural system, or the approaching storm clouds which would savagely open them up. He certainly would have been unaware of plague infested fleas from Central Asia which, carried in the fur of rats, would soon kill millions of already weakened peasants and lords alike. The story of these events and the resulting decline of villages will unfold in the next chapter.

STILL THERE
FEATURES TO LOOK OUT FOR

■ *FIG 2.21: ARLESCOTE, WARWICKS: Ridges and furrows. Note how the ridges in the centre background form a reverse S shape: see Fig 2.4 (see page 34).*

■ *FIG 2.22: DINTON, BUCKS: An elaborate Norman doorway with the distinctive zig-zag pattern around the outside. The semi circular carving of two beasts above the door is known as the tympanum.*

■ *FIG 2.23: EARLS BARTON, NORTHANTS: A remarkable 1,000 year old Saxon church tower with the vertical, horizontal and diagonal stone bands believed to be imitating timber work. The various types of openings can be found on other churches from this period, though it is exceptional to find them all together like this, while the long and short stones up the corners are common at this time but are rarely found today. Note that the battlements at the top and the clock are later additions.*

■ *FIG 2.24: SUTTON COURTENAY, OXON: A late Norman window. The interlocking arches at the top are a common decoration from this period while the glass in the window is of later date.*

■ *FIG 2.25: WING, BUCKS: Although at first glance a typical English church this building is believed in part to be 1,200 years old. The seven sided end of the chancel nearest to you is known as an apse and this one dates from the late 10th century. On its left face, just at ground level you can see the top of an arch which leads to the crypt beneath where Christian relics would have been stored, making this an important church in the Saxon period. The main body of the church with its distinctive tall nave is the oldest part although its antiquity is masked by the windows, battlements and a west tower of much later date.*

■ *FIG 2.26: STEWKLEY, BUCKS: A virtually unaltered Norman church dating from the middle to late 12th century, although originally the stone walls would probably have been rendered as in Fig 2.9 (see page 44). Note the typical Norman features of zig-zag patterns around the doors and windows and on the tower the interlocking arches above the blanked out openings, known as 'blind arcading'.*

■ FIG 2.27: GREENSTED, ESSEX: The vertical wooden timbers on the right of the picture are the only example of a Saxon wooden church in the country. The roof and porch are all much later while the timbers had their rotten bases cut off and the brick wall inserted beneath them during the Victorian restoration. The stone coffin lid enclosed in the railings dates from 1200, and is believed to have been for a bowman who lost his life in the Crusades.

■ FIG 2.28: YELDEN, BEDS: The remains of a motte and bailey castle dating from the mid 12th century. The mound to the right of the picture is the motte while the bank coming round from the left and into the foreground is the outer perimeter of one of the baileys.

■ *FIG 2.29: ASKHAM, CUMBRIA: An ancient green flanked by later houses. Note how the 19th century school in the middle of the photo has encroached onto the green.*

■ *FIG 2.30: THE LANGDALES, CUMBRIA: A pollarded ash tree, with its new growth of branches above the reach of the grazing livestock.*

■ *FIG 2.31: ASHDOWN PARK (NT), OXON: This low bank running from the foreground, through the fences left of centre, and then up the hill between the fields, is the remains of a deer park boundary (park pale). The interior of the park is to the right and there are the faint signs of the ditch which would have kept the animals within it on that side of the bank.*

■ *FIG 2.32: BISHOPSTONE, WILTS: The flat surface curving from the right of the foreground and on into the centre of the picture is a strip lynchet which probably was formed halfway down this slope for cultivation in the medieval period.*

■ FIG 2.33: TISSINGTON, DERBYSHIRE: Fonts are one of the pieces of church furniture which are retained even when a church is rebuilt. This 11th century example shows the cylindrical form which was typical of early designs and was decorated with carvings of men and beasts.

■ FIG 2.34: ICKLINGHAM, SUFFOLK: A rare example of a thatched church which was the most common form of roofing in the Saxon and early medieval period. Also note the elaborate Decorated style of tracery in the window to the right, which probably dates from the early 14th century.

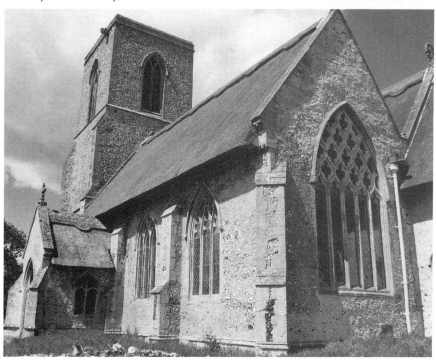

■ FIG 2.35: WHITELEAF, BUCKS: One way of identifying older roads and tracks is from their level compared with the surrounding land. Here the road has gradually cut into the soft chalk to form a holloway well below the level of the timber framed houses.

■ FIG 2.36: QUARRENDON, BUCKS: What at first glance appears to be just an old pond in the corner of a field is in fact a moat only a small part of which is still in water. Many old manor houses and countless farms are still surrounded by moats, some of which can date from the 12th-16th centuries. They may also indicate the site of a lost village, as in this case where on the hill beyond the largest tree is a mass of humps and bumps marking the old lanes and houses of a settlement long since abandoned.

CHAPTER 3
DECLINE AND DESERTION

The Later Middle Ages: 1300 to 1550

■ *FIG 3.1: The date is now 1500 and our imaginary village is showing signs of decline. The owner of the house which we saw being erected in the previous view has taken over the two plots next to him as they were deserted by their owners, and he has removed the buildings and turned the land over to crops. The market which was held on the green to the left was short-lived, and this grassy patch is only used by the remaining poor for their limited livestock to graze. The manor house and church have been enlarged mainly due to profits the lord has made from sheep farming, which on the hill in the distance has led its landlord to enclose the previous open fields for his flocks. The remaining part of our village which used to sprawl down to the river now comprises just a few larger houses, close by the mill, which has attracted employment as it has been converted from grinding grain to the fulling of wool.*

What has caused the turnaround in the fortunes of our village which when we last saw it was a picture of expansion and success? Why is the landscape around changing again, albeit to a more recognisable format, and why despite the obvious decline are there some who are clearly not short of a *penny or two? This chapter will look at the reasons behind these changes and describe how these affected the physical appearance of villages.*

THE NATIONAL PICTURE

The storm clouds which were mentioned at the end of the previous chapter finally broke over England in the early 14th century. Firstly there was a climatic downturn, often referred to as the Little Ice Age, which was to last until the 17th century, producing times of ice cold winters and wet ruinous summers. Harvests were poor and widespread famine affected the country particularly from 1315 to 1317. Yet worse was to come!

From Asia came rats which carried fleas infected with bubonic plague. The disease spread over Europe and entered England from the south coast in the summer of 1348. By December 1349 it is estimated to have claimed the lives of some 2-3 million people. It did not matter if you were rich or poor, the appearance of small black buboes (hence the Black Death, the common name for this first outbreak) on your body meant you might have only days to live. The plague also revisited these shores numerous times over the following three centuries, and the population continued to fall well into the 15th century. The fear and foreboding this created can be seen in the monuments, tombs and church architecture of the period.

The most notable effect of the Black Death was the change in social structure due to the scarcity of labour. There simply were not the numbers of people to work the land, so those who survived could demand more, or move to a different village where there might be a more progressive lord of the manor. Parliament tried to fix wages to previous levels, an impossible task that only increased tensions which after the imposition of a Poll Tax in 1380 erupted into the Peasants' Revolt. Labourers from Kent and Essex overran London, executed ministers and demanded the abolishment of the legal ties of servitude to their lord. The revolt fell apart after the death of Wat Tyler, one of its leaders, and any concessions from the King were promptly withdrawn. Despite its apparent failure the continuing shortage of labour meant that the following century would see wages rise and peasants able to escape from the humiliation of servitude which had been one of the rebels' objectives.

By the mid 15th century we had lost most of our French possessions, and there was widespread discontent with an inept monarchy. The resulting Wars of the Roses saw the ruling classes fighting for control, usually in small scale battles (with the exception of Townton) which had little effect on the life of village

■ *FIG 3.2: The line in our population chart suddenly drops at the time of the Black Death but continues downwards to a low of about 2-3 million before recovering in the 16th century.*

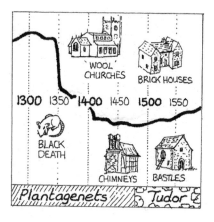

England. This period of disruption came to an end with the victory of Henry Tudor at Bosworth in 1485, and his subsequent dynasty saw in a period of stability and for the first time in more than a century a rising population. His son Henry VIII had a greater effect on village life when between 1536 and 1539 he dissolved the monasteries and claimed their property and revenue for the Crown. Not only would some villagers now find themselves with a new lord of the manor and the loss of income from servicing the old abbeys, but they would also have to change the very way they practised their faith.

AGRICULTURE

The worsening climate in the 14th century brought about crop failure and therefore famine. There were no European grain mountains or huge quantities of imported crops on which to fall back! The first to suffer from this initial blow would have been those forced to farm marginal lands like upland areas and moors where the weak, thin soils would have struggled to support a good crop even in better weather, and now they were abandoned.

The Black Death had an even more devastating effect. Initially it would have left the great open fields around the village only partly farmed, not a good situation as there was no physical boundary between your strip and one next to it now full of nettles and weeds. As a result most would have been taken over by neighbours that survived the epidemic, and they would have been encouraged to do so by their anxious lord. He relied on the income from his estate to keep him and his entourage in the manner to which they had become accustomed, and the last thing he wanted was to see land lying idle and unproductive. He might even try and poach labour from a nearby manor, offering peasants better conditions or even wages.

Some villagers soon realised that the tables were turning and they were now in a position to better their lot. If their lord of the manor decided it was best to lease or even sell his land, those ambitious villagers could buy it up and rise to join a new social rank, that of the yeoman farmer. These changes in land ownership began to alter the physical appearance of the countryside as fields and wastes were enclosed with hedges, fences and walls.

Enclosure by Agreement

This was the breaking up the old common fields and wastes into contained blocks of land held by one farmer, and would usually occur where there had been such a loss of life or people moving away that the land could be easily divided between the few remaining villagers. They would firstly have to group their holdings together as their arable strips were scattered at random around the open fields. Once they had bought and exchanged these between them, the new farmers could set about enclosing their consolidated holdings to form new fields, usually for cattle or sheep.

As the new holdings were made up of a collection of the old strips the new boundaries which the farmers erected around them would mirror the shapes they formed. As discussed in the previous chapter the strips either gently curved or made a reversed S shape (due to the method of ploughing) when looked at from the air. You may be able to recognise hedges today around your village which form these shapes on a map although they could date from any time between the 13th and 18th centuries. These early fields were often quite large, but were then later subdivided, and are often interlocked into patterns shaped by the earlier furlongs and strips.

These early enclosures seem to have occurred mainly in the west and north, in counties like Hereford, Shropshire, Cheshire and Lancashire, and also in parts of Suffolk, Essex and Kent. Where the common system of open fields was dominant, especially over the Midlands and up into Yorkshire, enclosure at this date is rare; the new farmers bought up abandoned strips but continued to farm as a community. It would have been too complicated especially if the village was well populated to enclose the fields with all parties reaching agreement. There were some exceptions: for instance when a farmer wanted to grow a different crop from the surrounding one in the open field, he could fence in his strip leaving long, thin fields which you can still identify today.

One sign to look for in fields containing grassed-over ridges and furrows which shows the process of buying up your neighbour's plot is when the ridge appears to rise, then kink as it falls and continues on a slightly different alignment. This shows where the farmer bought the next strip up, ploughed over the old headland between them, hence the rise and fall, then had to align the new ridges to his existing ones which led to the kink.

In the 15th century many landowners decided to change from arable farming to rearing livestock, especially sheep, due to the low labour cost and the rising price and demand for wool. This could be done with a greater profit by clearing the land of houses and their crofts, enclosing the fields and turning them over to pasture. These attempts to remove villages and enclose common land brought much protest especially in the Midlands, though it often still went ahead despite legislation, investigations and commissions. It also seems to have been prevalent in the wastes of the North and areas like Gloucestershire where sheep farming had always been an important part of the local economy.

Woodland

Although there was a general fall in population, there were areas like North Warwickshire where the forests were still being reclaimed for agriculture during this period. Other woodland was used in the same way it had been for centuries even where land was enclosed, as timber was still required for houses, and wood for fencing and heating. The old tale we were told at school, that the Tudors cut down great swathes of forest to build their navy, flounders when you realise they had to build but a few hundred ships, compared with the demand for hundreds of thousands of houses for the recovering population. Shipbuilding had more of an effect on our woodland in the late 18th century with the building of thousands of much larger craft for the Empire's growing Merchant and Navy fleets.

By the time that Henry VIII was selling off the lands of the monasteries, the country was losing its great open fields, farmers and farms had appeared, and large swathes of the countryside were dotted with flocks of valuable sheep. All the causes of these changes and the response of agriculture to adapt to them had a direct effect on the village around which they centered.

THE VILLAGE

When a major disaster strikes it is often found that the tragedy was caused not by one, but by a number of unfortunate events. If just the one fault had occurred the safety systems would have coped and the situation could have been recovered, but when two or three things go wrong at the same time then disaster is inevitable. It is very much the same with villages. If a village was struck by the Black Death then although weakened it would stand a good chance of recovery, but if this came after years of poor harvest, climatic change, then the return of the pestilence, or it became more profitable to use the land for sheep, then an already fragile community might vanish for good. Although a number of villages were deserted due to the Black Death, it is now clear that in many cases the settlements weakened by these events were not finally deserted until the late 14th and 15th centuries. So far some 3,000 deserted medieval villages (DMVs) have been identified.

The physical effect on the village of these events would therefore depend on its size and population. A larger settlement which maintained a good number of residents would show signs of decline in the form of abandoned houses and land between those which were still occupied. Over a period of time these may have been reoccupied by a neighbour who would take over or buy up the vacant plots. In this way the regular, planned layout of the 12th or 13th century village has become irregular and difficult to identify due to this later breaking up of the original plots.

The smaller, less populated settlements were more likely to succumb to desertion. This could be a gradual process spanning in some cases five or six hundred years until the final resident departed. In others the remaining population was simply uprooted to make way for sheep farming. Where the land on which these villages stood is now under the plough, then the only trace may be pieces of broken pottery which have been turned up by the farmer. Systematically walking across fields (fieldwalking) can identify areas of intense

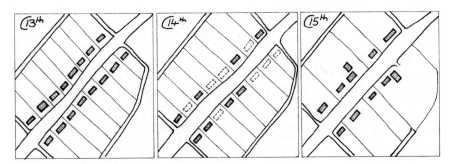

■ *FIG 3.3: Three plans of the same village over successive centuries with the grey rectangles representing the houses. In the first one is the freshly laid out, regular planned village, but in the second the houses marked by the dashed lines have been abandoned after the Black Death. In the last one the neighbours have bought out those vacant plots, removed the old houses and fences and have enlarged their farmsteads. This is an example of how a seemingly irregular village could have originally been planned.*

debris and hence relocate these lost settlements. In other cases the land has remained pastoral and the shape of the village can be recognised by the grassed-over raised platforms of the old houses. These were formed by the constant rebuilding of the houses (probably every 20 to 30 years) and the build up of general occupational waste. The roads and tracks which run between them are usually lower as the constant wear or removal of manure from its surface would have left them hollowed out (holloways). Villages in this situation are easier to find, some being marked on a 1:25 000 or larger scale Ordnance Survey map, or showing up on air photographs, while most can be recognised on the ground, especially in low winter sunlight.

As in previous periods there was a surprising amount of settlement mobility. Some villages may have drifted away from an area prone to flooding now the climate had deteriorated, or they moved onto better land which had been abandoned. In other cases whole villages were relocated on a nearby but new site, often due to the actions of the landlord but in others for reasons which remain to be discovered. Some settlements may have appeared near a new industrial area or developed along important roads to service the increasing amount of long distance travellers by the 16th century. Despite the population fall there were still some new settlements in parts of England, including some early coastal fishing villages.

THE VILLAGE ELEMENTS
The Church
Despite the decline in population and all the social and economic problems it caused, the 15th century was a good time financially for some of those who had survived. There were new opportunities, land was cheap and sheep were in demand, so the new breed of entrepreneurial individuals like merchants could make a fortune. Where as in previous centuries they would give their money to monasteries in order to assure them a safe passage to Heaven, they now directed their funds to the parish church. In areas of the country which benefited particularly from sheep farming, completely new or enlarged churches appeared, embellished in the latest Perpendicular architectural fashion. These so called 'wool churches' are a notable feature of areas like the Cotswolds, but reached their zenith in East Anglia where stunning edifices of glass and flint like Long Melford seem, and probably were, oversized ego trips which the entire village population would have struggled to fill!

■ *FIG 3.4: LONG MELFORD, SUFFOLK: This glorious church blessed with a profusion of glass was completed in 1484 thanks to the profits of local cloth merchants. At the right hand end is the lady chapel, an unusual feature on a church that was never an abbey or cathedral, while at the other end the stone tower dates from 1903 and encases a brick tower which had replaced the original one after it was destroyed by lightning around 1710.*

This was also a high point in the architectural development of the English church. Over many centuries and by trial and error rather than design, masons had made buildings larger, brighter and more elegant. Clever use of buttresses allowed walls to be thinner and a larger proportion of them could hold windows which now in richer churches had colourful displays of glass framed by flowing and then vertical styles of tracery. Roofs were flatter and were now covered in thinner materials like lead, while inside timber or occasionally stone vaulting was painted and adorned with mouldings, like angels. New west towers were built, sometimes replacing old central ones, while clerestories (a line of windows along the top of the nave) allowed extra light in to illuminate the colourful display of wall paintings. A timber rood screen with a crucifix mounted upon it would have separated the chancel, where the ceremonies were still conducted in Latin, from the nave, where the villagers still stood or, if they were lucky, sat on benches.

The upkeep of the nave was the responsibility of the parishioners, while the chancel came under the jurisdiction of the clergy. But while the wealthy local parishioners seemed happy to turn their part into a architectural masterpiece, the poor old clergy would do their best just to keep their section standing. This situation can still be seen today where a flat roofed nave usually with aisles either side meets a humble chancel which still retains the earlier steeper and often higher pitched roof (see Fig 3.31 - page 102).

Another addition to the church which was popular with the local lords was the chantry chapel. These were principally for the singing of the mass (chantry as in chanting, comes from the Latin word 'cantare' which means 'to sing') and prayers which were usually to the memory of the founder. They could be an additional building, either freestanding or affixed to the chancel, or they may have taken over an aisle within the church which would then be screened off. Within these they could bury the family members and worship at their own private altar. If you were in a particularly generous mood and incredibly wealthy at the same time, you could found a collegiate church. These were completely new or rebuilt edifices run by a group of secular clergy who would pray for the soul of the founder. The site would usually include a college building or grammar school for the education of a limited number of pupils and possibly an alms or bede-house for a selection of elderly or poor men. Both chantries and collegiate churches were suppressed at the Reformation, although some exceptional examples like Westminster Abbey survived.

Effigies on the tombs in this period would often take the classic medieval pose of the deceased, lying straight on his or her back, with hands held together in prayer. A more chilling and thankfully uncommon style which appears in the 15th century is a cadaver (a carving of the dead incumbent in a state of decay or as a skeleton!). These grotesque and realistic effigies can be found on their own or underneath one showing the deceased in healthier times, and may have been a pious act to demonstrate that whatever one's rank, death eventually comes to us all. This grim realism could also find its way onto brasses, although you are more likely to find ones picturing knights and lords in the fashionable pose of the day. The oldest surviving brasses date from the late 13th century, although the artwork is of such quality that they must have developed over some considerable time before.

These memorials held within the treasure house of your parish church are usually the first opportunity you will have to come face to face with those local historic figures which before this period are just lifeless names on old documents. Early effigies are not true representations of the deceased, but after the introduction of death masks in the later 14th century they become more accurate portraits. They are also fine works of art often by the top sculptors of the day and can be dated by the variety of fashions in poses and details. It was also the habit for great families to continue to bury their dead in the parish church of their ancestral home. So for instance at Chenies in Buckinghamshire there are the tombs of the Russell family, the Earls and Dukes of Bedford, despite the fact they left the manor in 1608 and moved firstly to Moor Park, Herts and then Woburn, Beds!

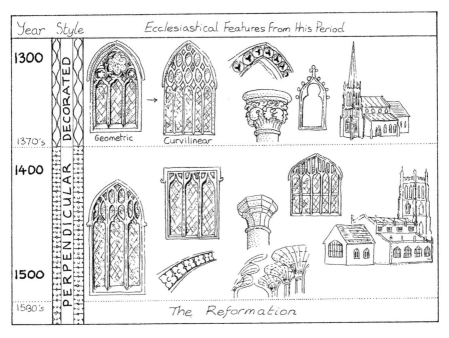

■ *FIG 3.5: A chart showing some of the features and styles of churches and the architectural style and date to which they belong. Note that many of these styles were copied or adapted in Victorian churches.*

Monasteries

The true reasons behind Henry VIII's decision to dissolve the monasteries are much debated. What is certain is that monastic life was in decline long before the Dissolution. The monks were just as affected by the catastrophes of the 14th century as other lords, their estates faced the same drop in revenue on which they were so reliant and their holy status was no protection against the ravages of the bubonic plague.

The monasteries also suffered from a change in the fashion of endowment. Whereas previously kings and lords had blessed them with tracts of land to support their extensive and expensive abbey buildings, the wealthy of the country were now building chantries and collegiate churches to guarantee their place in Heaven. To make matters worse there was a general concern among the people about the running of the Church. This grew into a disrespect for some sections of the clergy and manifested itself in many ways from the simple act of jeering right up to all out riots! Some even questioned the monks' rights to the very land they were so dependent upon. The indifference to monastic life which evolved mainly in the populous South of England made Henry VIII's Dissolution of the Monasteries that much easier, and his defeat of the opposition to it in the North ensured its swift completion.

Priories run by foreign churches, especially French ones, had already been suppressed in 1414 due to the Hundred Years War with France and the lands and funds in this case were directed back into the Church. At the Dissolution of the Monasteries though the Crown took all the rights and wealth of the abbeys and then granted the estates to favourites or sold them off. At a village level this would mean a new landlord and for those who had depended directly upon the monastery for employment or income, a worrying future. It also left a gap in the education system and in the support of the elderly and poor.

The Reformation

Henry VIII's marriage problems have been well documented and filmed. He basically wanted to rid himself of his first wife, Catherine of Aragon, who had failed to bear him a male heir, and marry his new love Anne Boleyn. Henry though complicated his attempts to gain a divorce by accusing the Papacy of error in granting dispensation for the original marriage. The outcome of the failure to resolve this dispute with the Pope was firstly the Submission of the Clergy in 1532 and then the Act of Supremacy of 1534, which in effect made Henry the head of the Church of England. The power gained was not only essential to sanction the Dissolution of the Monasteries, but also to permit the publication of the first Bible in English. As we will see in the next chapter the effect at a village level of Henry's actions was immense.

The Manor House

In deserted villages the manor house may have gone the way of all the other buildings, but in many it may have survived as a farmhouse. Where there was decline it could have been passed down to a yeoman farmer who had bought or rented the lord's demesne land. But where the manor house still fulfilled its role it saw expansion and division.

■ *FIG 3.6: AVONCROFT MUSEUM OF HISTORIC BUILDINGS: A 15th century house with the hall and its distinctive tall window and a jettied cross wing to the left of it. Note the louvre on the top right of the roof directly above the hearth which by the position of this opening tells you that the fire is no longer in the centre of the hall but has been moved next to the passage which runs from behind the doorway.*

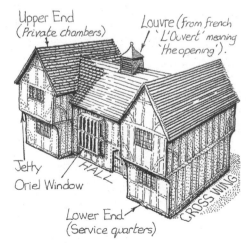

■ *FIG 3.7: A picture of a manor house and some of its features including an oriel window which projected from the wall and was popular in the 15th and 16th centuries.*

The lord of the manor now demanded some privacy and the open hall layout where the whole household slept together now seemed outdated, so this simple arrangement was expanded upon. The most common way of achieving this was by adding cross wings at one or both ends of the hall. These two-storey extensions would at the upper end (the lord's end) include his private chambers (solar), while the lower end (the service end) could contain a dairy, buttery and a storeroom above.

■ *FIG 3.8: WEALD AND DOWNLAND OPEN AIR MUSEUM: The interior of the hall of a 15th century house with the hearth in the bottom right corner and the two doors leading off to the service rooms.*

■ *FIG 3.9: AVONCROFT MUSEUM OF HISTORIC BUILDINGS: The interior of a service room. Note the shutter to the left of the open window which would have either slid on runners or would have been hinged.*

These wings would often have a jetty which from the outside would make the once dominant original hall look like an insignificant recess! Some of the best examples of these forms of houses are the Wealdens, so named after their popularity in the Weald of Kent and Sussex (see Fig 3.20 - page 97). In other designs the whole wing could stand out to form an L shape or C shape plan. As the wealth of other members of the village increased they also could expect a house along similar lines, especially by the 15th century.

The major factor in the development and hence investigation of old houses is the chimney. At first the central hearth was moved to an end of the hall either under a smoke hood, a timber-framed structure to trap the rising smoke and a notorious fire risk, or within a smoke bay, which was a walled off partition running across the hall. The appearance of the brick or stone chimney not only solved the fire risk problem but also allowed a floor to be inserted across the hall, a cheaper way of gaining extra rooms than building a new extension. The position of these new chimneys would also have an effect on the layout of the house and just by looking at where one is on the roof line can tell you a lot about the internal arrangement and date of old houses.

Brick Houses

From the departure of the Romans up until the 14th century all houses were made from timber, stone or cob, but now brick made a reappearance. There were a few buildings in the Saxon and medieval period that had reused the distinctive, flat bricks from ruined Roman buildings, but the knowledge of how to make them had gone with the withdrawal of the Empire way back in the 5th century. Now brickmakers from the Low Countries where the skills had not been lost were invited over to select the correct clay, make the clamps and oversee the firing. Many village accounts, mainly in the south and east due to their close proximity to Flanders and Holland, mention sums paid to '... the Flemynge ...' or '... the Docheman ...' recording the work done by Flemish and Dutch craftsmen.

There would not have been brickworks, rather the man whom the building was for would supply the suitable clay then arrange for the brickmaker to make them in the locality or actually on site. Gradually some areas would develop a more permanent industry but this would still depend on the availability of the correct clay near the surface; once this was exhausted the workers would move on. Similar skills were also used in the production of tiles either for roofs or decorative floor tiles usually for churches and abbeys. As these processes were expensive, bricks were considered a luxury item which should be displayed for all to see, although as it was often used where stone could not be found, some pieces were plastered over to imitate masonry. Therefore in this period they were only used to construct the buildings of the wealthy, or in smaller quantities for gateways, church towers, walls and chimneys.

It is possible to identify these early bricks from their size (they appear to be flatter than today's bricks, approximately 2-2½" thick) and from their irregular shapes, colours and textures. The fashions in bonding (the way the bricks are laid) also varied over the centuries and can help in the dating of a brick feature. These old bricks will also look weathered but be careful as most walls would have been repointed at some stage and the new mortar may disguise their antiquity.

Castles

By the 14th century the great but short era of castle building was drawing to a close. Many existing ones were expanded or rebuilt because they still retained some strategic, residential or judicial role. These though were usually associated with towns which had either grown up around the castle or were its reason for being in the first place.

■ FIG 3.10: HERSTMONCEUX CASTLE: A mid 15th century fortified manor house built in brick which with a moat and turrets was designed to look like a castle. It was rebuilt in the 1930s having previously been dismantled in the 18th century.

In the countryside the new castles of this period were usually residential as it was still the fashion to build imposing structures surrounded by a moat with a drawbridge. You can often recognise these fortified houses by their symmetrical fronts, the use of brick, and windows instead of a limited number of slits. The original motte and bailey castles and others used in the baronial troubles of the 13th century were by now falling into ruin and disuse, though as we shall see in the next chapter some would have an Indian summer!

Tower Houses

In the border regions in the North of England, a defensive type of house developed between the 12th and 16th centuries. The earliest ones were built for the upper end of the social order and would have stood within a walled enclosure like a castle, in which the locals and livestock could have sought refuge when a Scottish raid threatened. The tower would have had thick stone walls in a square or rectangular plan, with three or four storeys in height. Access was via a retractable ladder from a first floor doorway, with an internal staircase being the only way into the ground floor, which therefore must have been of limited use, while above would have been the private chambers.

By the 14th and 15th centuries lesser nobles and farmers were building modest versions with a door on the ground floor and the staircase usually in the corner, accessing the upper hall and chambers. Where these survive today they are referred to as 'pele towers'; their defended enclosures have often long since vanished and they are usually part of a later building.

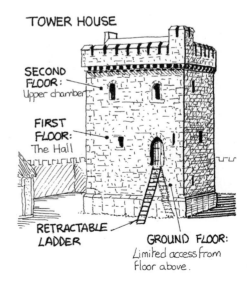

TOWER HOUSE

SECOND FLOOR: Upper chamber

FIRST FLOOR: The Hall

RETRACTABLE LADDER

GROUND FLOOR: Limited access from floor above.

■ FIG 3.11: A tower house as it may have originally appeared with the retractable ladder being replaced at a later date by permanent stairs.

Mills

The notable change to the mills in this period was the role they played rather than the buildings themselves. Windmills were still to develop into the structures we are familiar with today, but water mills were starting to be used for different purposes than just grinding grain. One of the important processes in turning wool into cloth is fulling, whereby the fibres of the newly woven cloth are compacted together by hammering. Numerous mills in the booming wool areas of the country, like the Cotswolds, were converted to power these hammers.

Inns and Tavern

Numerous pubs today claim the title of being the oldest in the country, usually tracing their heritage, or more often that of the building itself, back to the 14th or 15th centuries. The village pub as we know it did not exist at this date; most villagers would have brewed and consumed alcohol in their own houses.

The earliest inns were probably used by pilgrims as they were among the few who had any reason to travel great distances and therefore required accommodation and food. Many of these were associated with monasteries and abbeys, who were also great producers of ale and owned many inns and taverns. As long distance travel started to increase other groups like merchants required places to stay overnight, so the numbers of inns increased especially along the major long distance routes of the day. Although most inns date to the boom in coach travel of the 17th and 18th century, you may be able to trace some further back to this period. It is also possible that the village as a whole drifted over a number of centuries towards these new routes where new inns and shops could be established; another example of the mobility of settlements.

Peasants' Houses

As certain members of the community gained land and wealth they were able to build larger two-storey houses and it is these that along with the manor houses tend to be the only survivors in villages today, giving us perhaps a misguided impression of the quality of medieval life. The vast majority of the villagers were still living in humble longhouses of timber, cob or stone, with a thatched roof above and livestock within. Windows were open with just shutters or animal skins to keep out the draughts, and there were no chimneys with the smoke from the fire just drifting up through the rafters. There is, however, increasing evidence that the quality of these buildings was improving, so that the jump from this period to the 'Great Rebuilding' of the 16th century (see Chapter 4) was not as dramatic as previously thought.

■ *FIG 3.12: WEALD AND DOWNLAND OPEN AIR MUSEUM: An interior of a cottage with the hearth in the middle and a shutter across the window on the rear wall. This example has a dividing wall to the left though most cottages and longhouses would still have been open throughout in the 14th century.*

Ponds and Pits

It is often forgotten that there were small scale industrial workings throughout the Middle Ages. These were usually established near to where the required minerals, stones, clays and peat could be extracted easily from the ground.

The brick and tile making industries left areas of shallow pits where they had dug out the clay, and the numerous ponds around villages especially in the South and East may be remains of this industry. Clay was also used for cob walls, daubing infill panels and as a waterproof lining for manmade ponds, dams and riverbanks, so there may be pits nearby where this occurred. Lead and coal had been dug out or mined since Roman times, but now they were becoming more important as the former was required for the new flatter pitched church roofs and the latter was being transported by sea from the North East to London to meet the demands for fuel from the growing urban population. Groups or lines of what are known as bell pits, the remains of the top of the shafts dug to reach the seams, can be found mainly on moors and within woods in the coal and lead mining districts.

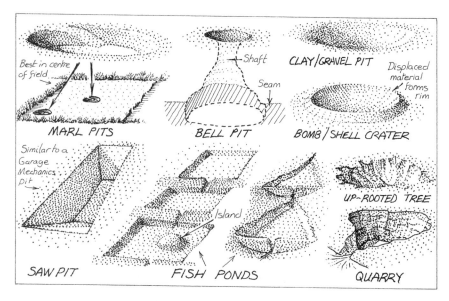

■ FIG 3.13: Some examples of pits and earthworks which you could find around your village today, and possible causes of them. Note that these are not to scale so, for instance, the saw pit which had to fit just one man within would be a lot smaller than the fish ponds or quarries which can cover acres.

East Anglia was probably the most populous area of England in the early medieval period, and due to the lack of woodland, peat was used for fueling fires. The huge amounts that were required inevitably led to the creation of massive pits, but where are they today? The answer is they are the Norfolk Broads! These popular waterways are the flooded pits created by medieval peat digging which died out in the 14th century due to rising sea levels. Pits were also dug near roads to extract stones for their repair, or sometimes they were even in them, the fines for which can be found in old manorial records. There would have been small quarries where stone was dug for local house building, but there were also areas where quarrying was an important industry even at this early date, especially where the stone was of a particularly good quality or uniqueness so that it was worth the considerable effort of transporting it out of the locality.

The different types of pits left by these workings around or within your village today may indicate the presence of one of these old industries, perhaps even the original reason behind the establishment of the settlement. Unfortunately it is usually impossible to confirm the exact reason for the formation of a pond or pit in its own right although documentary evidence or local names like Tylers Green or Kiln Cottage can help to confirm in this case the presence of tile manufacturing. It is also worth looking at parish boundaries; for instance if a number of them converge on a pond then this records the shared right of all these parishes to allow livestock to drink here and probably means the pond predates the laying down of these boundaries. In this case as in many others the ponds and pits are formed naturally by erosion or the actions of the last Ice Age, for instance sink holes and meres.

TRANSPORT
Roads and Bridges

As in the previous period there was no central body responsible for the upkeep of roads, so it was down to those in the locality to maintain them, or not as was often the case. Most local roads were no more than tracks with patches of gravel, stone or chalk filling up the worst of any pot-holes. By the 16th century though, travel on a national scale was gaining importance so soon something would have to be done to remedy the situation.

Bridges, on the other hand, like the churches and major houses of the period, were developing and were built of such quality that many survive today. These survivors are of stone, although timber bridges continued to be built. A common method of constructing a bridge would start with the preparation of the river bed, if necessary by driving a ring of wooden piles into it and filling in the enclosed area with rubble (a starling). The piers could then be built up on top of these with a pointed cutwater facing upstream, and in later bridges another one downstream (the triangular area above this would act as a refuge for pedestrians). The arches between the piers could be of three different types. Early ones may have been of a semicircular form as used in Roman, Saxon and Norman architecture, but any surviving bridges like this will be of a recent date when classic architecture was once again the fashion. The second type incorporated Gothic (pointed) arches which permitted greater height and easier passage of boats but required a large number of thick piers to support them. Greater flexibility came in the 14th century with the introduction of the segmented arch which was able to span wider spaces.

The building of a bridge was rarely completed in one go and this is one of the reasons why the piers are so thick as they possibly had to support an arch for a number of years before the remainder of the bridge was built. They also would have developed over time for, as mentioned in Chapter 2, they may not have had parapets originally or if they did, they might just have had a timber rail.

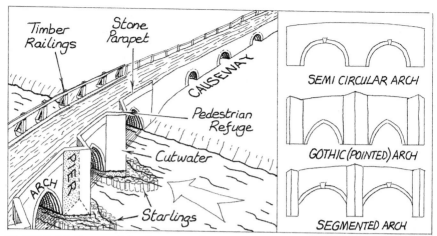

Labels within figure: Timber Railings, Stone Parapet, CAUSEWAY, Pedestrian Refuge, Cutwater, Starlings, PIER, ARCH, SEMI CIRCULAR ARCH, GOTHIC (POINTED) ARCH, SEGMENTED ARCH

■ FIG 3.14: Some of the features of a medieval bridge and elevations showing the three main styles of arches.

The stone walls which line the surviving bridges today could be a later addition, just as the pointed cutwaters, especially the downstream ones, may have been. Another important element used where a bridge crossed a flat flood plain was a causeway leading up to it. This could be just as impressive a monument as the bridge itself and would have had small arches of its own to let water pass under at time of floods.

There were numerous dangers on top of the seasonal condition of the roads in the Middle Ages and in order to bless the traveller, chantry chapels were often built on the bridges of the day. These would have usually been found on the major crossings in towns but there is evidence for some elsewhere. They were especially popular in the 14th century but as with other forms of chantry chapel they were robbed or demolished with the reforms of Henry VIII.

Large or numerous items went by cart, but smaller loads could be carried more economically in packs strapped over a horse's back. Where the routes they used crossed a river or stream a packhorse bridge may have been built, which are best perceived as smaller, thinner versions of their wider counterparts. They were important even in good weather as horses can have the irritating habit of wanting to roll about in the water to cool down, which would not have done the packs they were carrying much good! The packhorse bridge could also be constructed with a steeper incline leading up to it than ones which carried carts.

Your village today may stand near a medieval bridge, the history of which may be wrapped up in its architecture, especially under the arches where you can often identify later road widening from the original span (see Fig 3.22 - page 98). They were also major financial projects so records may exist about its construction or funding. It is worth noting that bridges were still the least common method of crossing a river, and you are more likely to find a ford or ferry in this period. It was (and still is) not unusual to find a ford and bridge side by side, as the use of the ford when the weather was good would have cut down on the wear and tear of the bridge and perhaps have avoided a toll. It is possible to find evidence for a ford not so much by any physical remains (cobbles under a bridge may be a method of protecting the piers which later replaced starlings and not an old ford) but by the widening of the boundaries on one side, revealing the old route to the crossing.

THE VILLAGERS

Tombs, sculpture, graffiti and documents tell us that the fear of death was never far from the minds of villagers throughout the 14th and 15th centuries. As previously mentioned though, the survivors from the catastrophic and repeated outbreaks of plague were in a stronger position than their predecessors. Labour shortages led to an increase in wages and these could be spent buying up abandoned plots or leasing land from the lord's demesne. Some of this new breed of ambitious peasant rose in standing to become yeoman farmers or husbandmen while in a few cases they even climbed the social ladder and became regarded as gentry!

This acquisition of land was made possible by changes in tenancy agreements forced on the landlords by the difficulties in retaining workers, and by a decline in the practice of passing down property by inheritance to family members. So rather than working your lord's land in return for a sustenance living, you could now escape this feudal system, and farm your own holdings to try and make a profit for yourself. These villagers could also supplement their income by offering their services for seasonal or part time employment. This could include brick and tile manufacturing, quarrying and mining, the building of houses and barns, iron working, and breeding and selling rabbits and fish. If you owned a cart or plough you could lease them out, while other members of the household could bake bread or brew beer to sell to the increasing numbers of travellers. Within your own croft you could grow apple, plum, cherry and pear trees, plant vegetables, peas and beans, and even humble grass for use as fodder.

■ *FIG 3.15: An imaginary late 15th century village scene. You can just make out the earthworks of former houses on the hilltop behind the plume of smoke, and the land here and along the top of the hill has been turned over to large fields of grass for sheep. Despite the village below having shrunk in size there are now a number of larger houses like the two-storey one to the left, while the church has been rebuilt in the latest Perpendicular style.*

Although this is a period when much of the land either lay abandoned or was converted to pasture, there was still money to be made from growing crops. In the areas where massive flocks roamed fields of grass, people would still have to eat, so the arable farmer would have a regular market for his produce and an ample supply of manure! In other, especially upland, areas where some craft and industrial work was becoming full time, someone would still have to grow corn within or supply it from outside the village. This picture of success was in this period the luxury of the minority, and the general theme of decline, desertion and death loomed over the average villager, as they still found themselves bound to or contented to stay in the village of their birth.

SUMMARY

The regional split of the previous period between the great open fields of the lowland areas and the upland pastures was always fragmented by regional anomalies. Now as more individuals became responsible for the land and how it was farmed, this split becomes more confused and it should never be assumed that just because your village lies in a certain part of the country that it would have looked the same or worked in the same way as the neighbouring settlements. The way the land was held, the whims of individual lords, the local geology, the presence of a town, road or river - all played their part in making your village unique.

The countryside around was also changing; it must have looked more ragged with abandoned plots and strips filled with nettles, contrasting with fields of neatly cropped grass sprinkled with flocks of sheep. Fences and hedges appear enclosing them or just individual blocks within the great arable fields. The village at the centre of all this would also be changing. The regular layouts of those which had been planned were being broken up, while all villages were suffering from varying degrees of abandonment. There would have still been hovels owned by the very poor, but now new two-storey houses of the yeomen and husbandmen would rise above them, the village gaining a more pronounced third dimension.

We know more about this period than those before due to the increase in the written word. This is the time of Chaucer's *Canterbury Tales*, the *Paston Letters*, Caxton's printing press and the translation of the Bible. Culturally the people of this land were thinking of themselves as part of an English nation rather than a European empire. English, which had been the language of the masses, had now replaced French in the court of the monarch, and was competing with Latin in literature and education. We were for the first time in the 16th century under the rule of a single monarch responsible for our island alone, and this awareness of nationality would be further crystallised in the following period by our military endeavours in defending the realm.

A villager looking out across his land in 1550 may have admired his own ingenuity in acquiring land and a social standing his ancestors would never have even dreamed of. His neighbour, on the other hand, may have been full of foreboding as the threat of plague was still prevalent, the markets in which he now traded were prone to fall as well as rise, and the church and religion which was the bedrock of his family life was suddenly entering an unknown future. From this uncertainty would emerge in the next period the successful, entrepreneurial gentry and farmers while at the other end of a widening social spectrum in the village, the humble peasant living at a sustenance level on the diminishing common land would face poverty and eviction.

STILL THERE
FEATURES TO LOOK OUT FOR

■ *FIG 3.16: LAVENHAM, SUFFOLK: This famous village bursting with timber-framed buildings was in fact a thriving town at its peak in the 15th century when it was a centre for the local cloth industry. Unfortunately the town had no major water source - required for later fulling mills - which meant it lost out to competition from northern and western areas in the 17th century, nor was there coal locally for the steam engines which powered the mills in the 19th century. A case of a village's decline being a result of its local geology.*

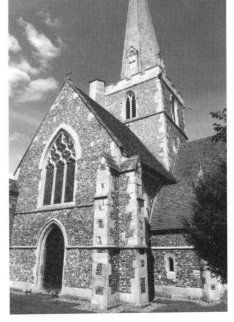

■ *FIG 3.17: SHOTTESBROOKE, BERKS: Built in the mid 14th century as a collegiate church it has survived without any major later additions. As the college was a religious foundation it was dissolved by Henry VIII and most of its buildings and those of the village which stood next to it have now gone.*

■ *FIG 3.18: LUDGERSHALL, BUCKS:*
The standard styles of capitals,
fonts and monuments within a
church can be assigned to a
certain period but there are also
many distinctive variations
produced by a sculptor who in
those days only worked within a
local area. This capital has
peasants with interlocking arms
and comes from the mid 14th
century.

■ *FIG 3.19: BINHAM, NORFOLK: All that remains today of this Benedictine*
priory after its dissolution apart from the remains of its buildings in the
foreground is, behind them, the nave of the old priory church which was
retained for use by the local parishioners.

■ *FIG 3.20: WALTHAM ST LAWRENCE, BERKS: A Wealden house (so named after their popularity in the Weald of Sussex and Kent) with its distinctive central recess, which is believed to date from the 14th century. The house was given in 1633 to the poor of the village, then only later became an inn, an example of the caution which should be taken in assuming a pub must be as old as the building itself.*

■ *FIG 3.21: STOPHAM, SUSSEX: A medieval bridge dating from the early 14th century when it replaced an earlier timber one. The raised central arch is to allow small boats to pass beneath.*

■ *FIG 3.22:*
WALLINGFORD,
OXON: A detail
of Wallingford
Bridge showing
the earlier
medieval arch
beneath the
later and wider
Georgian one.
This was also
the place where
King Stephen
laid siege to
Queen Matilda
in the 12th
century civil war
mentioned in Chapter 2.

■ *FIG 3.23: THORNBOROUGH, BUCKS: Faint marks on this hillside just outside the village of Thornborough reveal the presence of a now deserted village site. In the top left part you can see the curving ridge and furrow marks, while the trench which runs up to the trees in the middle, then turns left up between the ridges and the farmhouse, is one of the roads alongside which the houses stood. This could be the original village of Thornborough which later moved to a new site, or perhaps the village just contracted leaving this deserted part, or was this a completely separate manor?*

■ *FIG 3.24: FULBROOK FARM, BUCKS: The earthworks in the field mark the site of a deserved medieval village which is miles from any remaining village. These often overlooked earthworks are in effect a plan of a lost settlement frozen in time, in some cases for up to seven hundred years!*

■ *FIG 3.25: EWELME, OXON: Brasses can date back to the late 13th century though this example commemorates John Spence who died in 1517. Ewelme church is part of a 15th century complex of almshouses and grammar school of which John Spence was master and here he is depicted in his academic dress.*

■ *FIG 3.26: EWELME, OXON: This highly decorated tomb with an effigy of the Duchess of Suffolk in prayer on top has a morbid underbelly. Look carefully through the traceried windows at the base and you can see a sculpture of the partly decomposed body of the deceased, a pious image known as a cadaver from a time when death was never far from the mind.*

■ *FIG 3.27: EWELME, OXON: Most medieval stained glass had been smashed by the end of the Commonwealth in 1660. Later restorers often found the fragments outside the church where they had fallen, and reset them in a window to make a random pattern like this one which contains bits dating from when the church was built in the 1430s.*

■ FIG 3.28: CHECKENDON, OXON: The interiors of medieval churches were embellished with colourful paintings which were whitewashed over after the forming of the Church of England. Much of this artwork, like this fragment, has been uncovered by 19th and 20th century restorers.

Fragments of 13th wall painting, Checkendon.

■ FIG 3.29: ASHWELL, HERTS: These carvings of 1361 in the tower of the church of Ashwell are a testimony to the chilling events of the mid 14th century. The theme of these lines is that 'a pitiable, fierce, violent' plague (the Black Death outbreak of 1349-50) had left 'a wretched populace' which was then struck by 'a mighty wind' (recording the storm of January 1361 which also blew down the spire of Norwich Cathedral). There is a full translation in the pamphlet 'Medieval Drawings and Writings in Ashwell Church, Hertfordshire'.

■ FIG 3.30: TISSINGTON, DERBYSHIRE: The low thorn hedge running up the middle of this picture is actually following the line of earlier ridges and furrows which you can just make out running down the hill from the foreground. The hedge forms the top half of the reverse S shape which was created by the procedure of turning the plough team on a medieval strip.

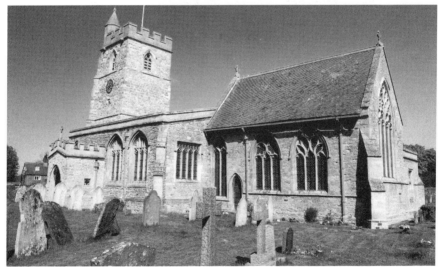

■ FIG 3.31: GREAT HORWOOD, BUCKS: The 14th century chancel on the right with its steep pitched roof and flowing, decorated tracery in the windows was not rebuilt when the nave, with its flat pitched roof and Perpendicular windows, was in the 15th century. This is often because the clergy who were responsible for the chancel did not have the funds compared with the congregation who would have paid for the rebuilding of the nave.

■ *FIG 3.32: LONG MELFORD, SUFFOLK: Although this dates from the later 16th century, it does contain many of the features of Tudor gate-houses such as, for instance, the use of brick and the octagonal towers, which were appearing in villages at the entrances to manor houses and castles.*

■ *FIG 3.33: CAREBY, LINCS: This picture shows how even when a bridge has been provided, the old ford alongside is still used. Even where the ford has not survived, the line of hedges can reveal where it used to cross.*

■ *FIG 3.34: GARSINGTON, OXON: Most medieval crosses which had stood over churchyards and market places were pulled down after the Reformation. It is quite common to find their stepped, stone bases still intact, with, in some cases, a replacement shaft and cross having been added in the 19th or 20th centuries. In this picture you can just make out the start of the original octagonal shaft on top of the rough stone steps and directly below its much smaller, later replacement.*

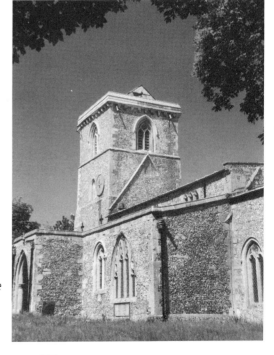

■ *FIG 3.35: BLEDLOW, BUCKS: The diagonal lines of masonry on the tower and to the right of the nave clearly mark the former higher pitched roof line.*

CHAPTER 4
EMPARKMENT AND ENCLOSURE

The Tudor, Stuart and Georgian Age: 1550 - 1800

■ *FIG 4.1: It is now 1800 and the industrial age has dawned. On the hill in the distance a local lord has built his new mansion on the side of the hill and has converted the old fields into a sweeping landscape park. The village on top of the hill was removed and just the remains of its once spired church have been retained as a romantic folly to be viewed up an avenue of trees from his house. To the right, down on the river, the fulling mill with its chimney has expanded and a new wharf has been built on the canal which now passes this side of it. The village has drifted down towards these sources of employment leaving the older part in the foreground on the outskirts of this re-expanding settlement. In front of us the exterior of the church has changed little while the manor house to the left has been rebuilt a number of times. The high wall on the right encloses the garden of the new rectory, but still retains the shape of the two medieval crofts which had been taken over by their neighbour in the previous view. On the site of his house now stands a new stone cottage which the man across the road can only look at enviously. His own timber-framed house, covered in a protective plaster layer, was built some years before on the old green, the only part of which still remaining is the pond by the T junction.*

In what are now comparatively recent times there have been dramatic changes in the surrounding landscape and to the buildings within our imaginary village. The scene is far more familiar to us now and has developed those attractive features that so endears the English village to us. Yet under this seemingly idyllic setting there is still poverty, discontentment and decline. This chapter will uncover the people who created this new picture, the reasons behind their actions and why it would lead to the ruin and eviction of so many villagers.

THE NATIONAL PICTURE

This is a period of English history dominated by the development of the Anglican Church amid fears of a Catholic revival. When Henry VIII died his son Edward accelerated reform of the Church along Protestant lines, only for his premature death to bring a vengeful and openly Catholic Mary to the throne. Her extreme measures of reversing the changes of Henry and Edward included burning up to three hundred future martyrs at the stake. She also alienated the now important landowning class who had no intention of handing back the confiscated church lands which they had been granted or had bought from Henry. Her actions planted the seeds of fear in the mind of the English, which were intensified when the Catholic King of Spain sent his ill-fated Armada in 1588 to remove the Protestant Elizabeth from the throne, or when the Gunpowder Plot to blow up her successor James I was uncovered in 1605. Many English manor houses contain secret passages, priests' holes or just the legends of them dating from the resulting persecution of the Catholics.

The new Church of England had problems at the other end of the religious spectrum from those who wanted to take reform to extreme lengths. These groups had equally rough treatment and included the Quakers, many of whom left on ships like the *Mayflower* for the American colonies, and the Puritans who more importantly made up a large part of the gentry class and hence Parliament. Their distrust for King Charles I and his Catholic wife, heightened by his demands for money to finance a war with the Scots which he himself started, helped to take England over the brink and into civil war. With battles and numerous skirmishes all over the country, opposing armies trampling crops and requisitioning livestock, the loss of life and rifts opening up between members of the same family, this conflict affected everyone down to the humble villager.

Although the monarchy was restored in 1660, the influence of Parliament had grown, so that by the end of the 17th century it had regular elections and positions of office for the landowning classes to fill. Ever since the Tudor period their numbers had greatly increased along with their wealth, based mainly on rents from their estates. There were new baronets, somewhere between the lords and the knights and below these the gentry, who were often richer than those above. Their new role in government brought in additional income, which along with speculating in joint-stock companies, exploiting mineral resources on their land and agricultural improvements on their estate made them even wealthier. Rather than spending their money embellishing churches as their predecessors had done, and which was now forbidden, they built themselves great mansions filled with treasures from all over Europe and surrounded by huge landscaped parks. A new consumer market appeared and the rich had money to spend on leisure and the arts.

The 18th century wasn't all roses to the upper classes, the collapse of the South Sea Company in 1720 left many a gentleman broke and agricultural depression up to 1760 reduced incomes from their estates. The improvements they made to maintain and raise this revenue had the effect of depriving the poorest in the village of what land they could use and many of the resulting destitute and evicted peasants became the new labour force in the towns. The Industrial Revolution may never have happened was it not for this spare labour and the increased productivity of agriculture.

Although visually some villages gained many of their attractive buildings and features in this period, in others the population continued to decline and in some cases complete desertion still occurred. The fate of the village and the villagers in the 17th and 18th centuries was a story of the land which surrounded them, and its emparkment and enclosure.

■ FIG 4.2: The line representing the national population shows the rising numbers in the Tudor times, a levelling off during the following period and then the sudden rise from 1760 due to a higher birth rate and a lower death rate. The population was around 9 million in 1800.

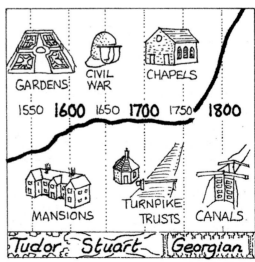

AGRICULTURE

During this period there were rises in the population which demanded additional food production and encouraged farmers to put new fields under the plough and to look at ways of increasing their productivity and hence profit. The 17th and 18th centuries were a time of great innovation - experimentation although not always implementation - from new agricultural tools to Jethro Tull's seed drill which produced more economical sowing. There were new crops and ways of rotating them in the fields, in particular the use of root crops for animal feed, and clover which returned nitrogen to the soil to increase fertility. The larger number of animals which could now be fed produced more manure which would enrich the fields for the next crop. These ideas all played their part in changing agriculture from husbandry, the caring and nurturing of the land, into farming for a profit.

Another important component in increasing productivity and profit would be to enlarge the amount of land under the plough. During the 17th century there was a resurgence of land reclamation from woods, heaths, moorland and most famously from the drainage of areas like the Fens. Here the Duke of Bedford and his group of adventure capitalists employed the Dutch engineer Vermuyden to build channels and drains in Cambridgeshire, Lincolnshire and Norfolk, and make the land suitable for farming. Unfortunately the drying peat soil shrunk and the land level dropped below that of the rivers which were meant to be draining it. Windmills powering pumps and new channels were built to solve the problem, but this area is still unnaturally lower than sea level. Names like Bedford Channel and fields called 'Adventurers' Lands' record the culprits for posterity.

Where this reclamation occurred new hamlets and villages could be founded especially where the clearance was associated with industry, mining or quarrying. Existing settlements would also be affected, with new buildings and farms but also with the loss of traditional trades associated with the previous landscape. You could also in the case of wetland areas find the river which ran through your village diverted around it in a new channel, leaving wide streets and even bridges as a reminder of its previous course.

Finally it was also believed that these new practices of rotation and mixed farming would work best within enclosed fields. Generally in the West, North and South East of England the open fields had either never existed or were already being enclosed by agreement. In the central band of the country from Wiltshire, up through the South and East Midlands and on into Yorkshire the open fields still dominated and efforts to enclose them met with strong opposition or the complication of there being too many landholders involved to come to an

■ *FIG 4.3: CROWLAND, LINCS: A 13th century three-legged bridge in the middle of this Fenland village which when the local river was diverted by a drainage scheme from its route along the streets was left high and dry! The statue on the bridge is believed to have come from Crowland Abbey sometime after its dissolution.*

agreement. Even here though in the common fields new crops and rotation were experimented with, the traditional three great fields were subdivided and new farming ideas applied. However, the pressure to enclose became too great with the sudden upsurge in the population from 1750, so the landlords and enterprising farmers looked to their friends in Parliament to authorise enclosures.

Parliamentary Enclosures had first occurred in the early 17th century, but between 1750 and 1850 they dramatically increased to change the whole landscape of the heart of Village England. The enclosure of a parish would usually be granted as long as those who applied owned the majority of the land there, whereupon a commissioner would be appointed. His task would be to divide up and reallocate the land with some respect to the farmers' previous holdings. Those with sizable claims would find a new set of fields clustered together rather than sprinkled randomly over the parish, while those with small holdings could lose out altogether and end up as landless labourers. The result of the commissioners' work often changed the social structure of the village while the surveyors' endeavours altered its physical appearance.

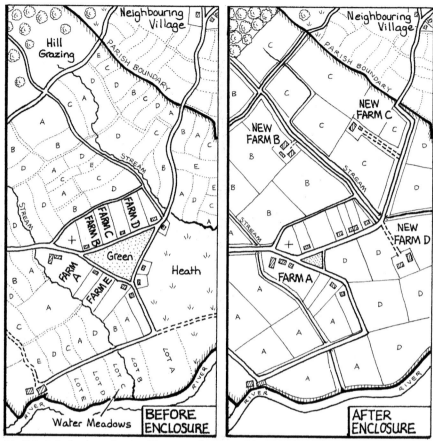

■ FIG 4.4: An imaginary village and most of its parish, before and after its Parliamentary Enclosure. The letters A-E in the fields show which ones belong to which farm. In the left hand map they are scattered across the open fields while in the right hand one they have been consolidated around the new farms. Note that Farm E who only had a small holding before has sold his land at enclosure and that Farm A remains in the village. The old heath and water meadows have been enclosed, as has most of the green. Also note the old road to the neighbouring village in the top right corner has been straightened, requiring a sharp left and right turn for it to line up with the road in the next parish which has not been enclosed yet.

Enclosures by Agreement had often resulted in new hedges and fences following the gentle reversed S shape of the old fields or the shape of existing features. With Parliamentary Enclosures the surveyors ruthlessly ignored the previous layout and laid down grids of straight hedgerows usually made up of hawthorn or blackthorn. Inevitably the roads between the fields would change which could mean when they reached the boundary of the parish they would have to be realigned by a set of sharp turns with the road to the next village (see Fig 4.4). These new roads are typically straight and set in a wide gap between the hedges with grass verges and ditches either side. It was also more economical for the farmer to establish home in the centre of his new holding rather then living in his old building back in the village. The architectural dating of these new isolated farms may help you uncover when the enclosure took place, although there are usually good records and maps produced by the commissioners and surveyors still available which can give a snapshot of your village two hundred years ago.

The houses the farmers left behind in the village were often split up to provide accommodation for the labourers who, now dispossessed of land, relied on their former neighbours for work. Their plight had been made worse because the commissioners also enclosed heaths, meadows, greens and other wastelands which the poor peasant had used to graze his few livestock or wildfowl, and from which he had gathered materials that were essential to his family's existence. Now with this income gone he could either become a wage-earning labourer, leave the village and set up home on some piece of unenclosed wasteland or, as thousands did, head off to the new industrial towns and cities and work in the factories. Some villages maintained or even grew in population depending on the success of the new farms and the markets they were now working for. In other villages enclosure may have played a part in their continued demise.

Upland Enclosures

The other areas affected by Parliamentary Enclosure in the late 18th and early 19th century were the commons and wastes especially in the upland regions like Northumberland and the old Lake District counties of Westmorland and Cumberland. These previously open moors and mountains were covered in an unsympathetic grid of dry stone walls which we now take for granted as part of the northern scene. In these parts the changes were less dramatic as these lands were only good enough for pasture although burning and reseeding could help improve them. Barns were built out in the new fields but the farms would usually remain in the village or hamlet. Some of the last Royal Forests, like Exmoor, were also enclosed at this time as well as many of the heaths of southern England.

Water Meadows

One problem with rearing sheep is feeding them in winter and especially at lambing time in March. Water meadows beside a river or stream were an answer to this. A thin layer of water was directed over the field, protecting the grass from frost and permitting an early growth for the flocks to feed on. Drains, sluices and ridges with channels down their spine are remains which you may find today around your village, particularly in southern England.

Woodland

The increased encroachment saw the demise of numerous woods in the 18th century. A curved or irregular shaped area divided up into small fields may indicate a former wood (and also a medieval deer park). Other woods were enclosed or converted to timber production, their more natural mix of flora and fauna being sacrificed in preference for the growth of one particular tree. Industry and mining also played their part in the decline of semi natural woodland although many still managed the trees with coppicing and replanting, to maintain their supply of fuel.

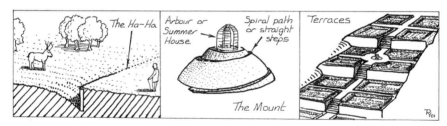

■ *FIG 4.5: Three features whose earthworks can still be found on land which was formerly a garden. The ha-ha was designed so that the lord standing to the right would see a continuous sweep of lawn, while the deer looking the other way is faced by a wall which it cannot cross.*

Emparking

By the mid 16th century the gentry had stopped spending money raising personal armies or embellishing local churches; now their status would be reflected in the great mansions and gardens towards which they directed their funds. The garden became for the first time an important part of these estates, intended to impress the visitor and in some cases royalty rather than being just a small area within which to promenade or grow a limited range of plants. These later Tudor gardens were influenced by the Renaissance and would usually have a rectangular area enclosed by a bank with the internal space set out in blocks

■ *FIG 4.6: POWIS CASTLE, POWYS: A view showing many elements from a late 17th century garden. The terraces were cut out of the rock sometime around 1700 and are shown with statues and low hedges around planting schemes and along with the formal garden in the middle distance are typical of the period. The sweeping park beyond merges with the distant countryside while the clump of trees to the right are part of a crescent shaped wilderness from which views could be gained over the garden.*

of low hedges containing geometric designs. The patterns were intended to be viewed from above, so a mount sometimes with a timber shelter on top was raised as a viewing point while outside the garden the old deer park would act as a tree-filled backdrop.

In the late 16th and early 17th centuries gardens were to become influenced by the latest French, Dutch and Italian designs. The general scale increases and features like terraces, topiary, statues and water features appear, although the designs are still very geometric. By the 1730s though a new movement towards a naturalistic landscape, inspired by the paintings of classic mythology by artists like Claude, resulted in the laying out of parkland with carefully positioned clumps and bands of trees, serpentine lakes, follies and temples. Gone are the flower beds and terraces, now sweeping lawns draw the eye over idyllic settings designed by famous gardeners like Capability Brown in which the wealthy could entertain and impress their guests.

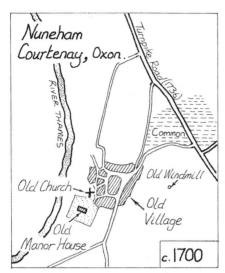 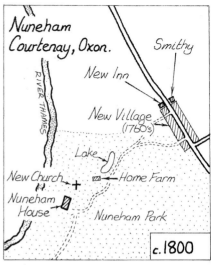

■ FIG 4.7: NUNEHAM COURTENAY, OXON: A map showing this village before
and after the estate was emparked. The old village was removed as part of
the landscaping of Nuneham Park in the 1760s and brick houses were
built along the new turnpike road for the dispossessed villagers, together
with an inn and smithy. It is possible that Nuneham Courtenay was in
Oliver Goldsmith's mind when he wrote the poem 'The Deserted Village'.

The problem which often faced these ambitious gentlemen was that the old
village which their ancestor's or predecessor's house had been within was now
in the way of their charming new gardens. They could hardly create a classic
landscape fit for the Gods, with a cluster of timber cottages and peasants in the
foreground! The result was that the emparking of these estates often included
the partial or complete removal of a village. There was no guarantee that the lord
in question would provide a purpose built settlement for the dispossessed
peasants and farmers, although by the later 18th century many did. These estate
villages usually built in brick or stone offered a better standard of
accommodation, although the reasoning behind these improvements was often
to present a picturesque approach to the estate for visiting gentry rather than
benevolence towards the villagers.

Estate villages are among some of our most attractive, although the hordes of
tourists which delight in their quaint and rustic features are often unaware of their
relatively recent origins. They can usually be recognised by a uniformity of
architecture, the use of the same building material throughout and if they are still
part of a working estate they may have the same colour front doors!

THE VILLAGE

Those villages which had survived the hard times of the 14th and 15th centuries could see regrowth as the population recovered and then boomed. This would often take the form of encroachment into areas like the green and other common land (see Fig 2.29 - page 66). Villages could also be further influenced by the presence of a new industry, road or canal. These could result in the gradual shifting of a settlement away from its original core and towards the new source of commercial opportunity, or the appearance of a completely new village. In the case of industry they may have been rather scattered affairs as it was only towards the end of this period that any factory or mine owner saw the benefits of housing their workers in a planned and well-built settlement.

We see in this period a resurgence in the foundation of new villages, whether as the result of reclamation, emparking, industry or transport. The effect of these and the Parliamentary Enclosures upon an existing settlement caused just as dramatic a change to both its physical layout and social order, the results of which are still evident today in the components of the village, or in the earthworks of those which declined.

THE VILLAGE ELEMENTS
The Manor House

The role of the manor house as the centre of the village, the place where the agricultural calendar was planned and from which judgements were cast, was to change from the Tudor times. If the village retained its open field system then these organisational duties may have lasted longer, but where the fields were enclosed into private holdings the farmer could make his own decisions independently of his neighbour, and new bodies could take over the other responsibilities. The Manor House becomes the grand home of the dukes, baronets, lords and gentry with its physical appearance and fashionable decoration designed to impress their ever increasing guest list.

Although many lords had previously moved their house away from the muddy lanes at the centre of their settlements, it was common during this period for the new mansions to be built within great parks at a comfortable distance from the village. There are numerous situations today where there is an old timber-framed or stone building dating from the 13th to 16th centuries and perhaps still called The Manor House within the village, while on the outskirts is the 17th or 18th century mansion which superseded it.

Many of these new buildings were no longer vernacular, that is made from locally available materials by local craftsmen, but became what is termed as 'polite architecture', reflecting fashions from the continent and being designed by the new breed of architects. Timber-framed masterpieces like Little Moreton Hall were superseded by stone and brick mansions, often E shaped in plan and with impressive displays of glass windows. By the mid 17th century steep pitched hipped roofs with a line of dormer windows overhanging a flatter, classic facade of usually five or seven bays became common, until they in turn were replaced in the 18th century by Palladian palaces adorned with parapets and columns.

There would usually be other buildings around the house, the most common would be a courtyard surrounded by stables and a coach house often given the same classical architectural treatment as the house itself. There may have been a church or chapel close at hand, perhaps the edifice from the displaced village or in some cases a completely new structure, sometimes in the form of a classical temple. Out of view of the house would have been the Home Farm, perhaps a keeper's cottage, as well as the stables and kennels for the lord's hunting horses and dogs. At the entrance to the estate there would be an elaborate gateway and probably a matching pair of lodge houses.

■ *FIG 4.8: LITTLE MORETON HALL, CHESHIRE: The famous moated manor house with its bold display of decorative timber-framing. The line of windows on the top floor is the Long Gallery, a popular feature in the 16th century.*

■ FIG 4.9: CASTLE HOUSE, BUCKINGHAM: The south front dating from 1708, displaying many of the features typical of a large late 17th century and early 18th century house.

Follies

We tend to use this term to describe elaborate or expensive buildings for which we see no purpose and therefore assume their construction was in folly. The scattering of classic structures we can still see around 18th century landscape parks today are often grouped into this category. These so-called follies though did have a purpose and were essential ingredients in any of these large garden schemes.

The paintings which had inspired the creating of these classic landscapes used ruined temples, romantic towers and crumbling arches to frame the foreground or act as a distant eyecatcher. The architects of the new gardens used either existing buildings, suitably rusticated and embellished, or constructed new temples, towers, sham castles and arches for the same effect. Their purpose therefore was primarily as part of a composition, but they usually had a secondary use for instance to house a collection, hold secret meetings, or simply from which to admire the estate. Grottos were another fashionable feature dating from the late 17th century, which would often take the form of a shell-lined cave by a lake, surrounded by trees, and perhaps even with a resident hermit.

These mysterious garden features often have their own local myths and there may be many stories relating to them that can be uncovered within the village. Also as these old estates become reclaimed by farmland, built over by roads and housing or sold off for other uses, the follies are suddenly rediscovered by the public and become a notable landmark around the village.

■ *FIG 4.10: BRADGATE PARK, LEICS: A folly known as Old John which dates from 1786. As is typical with follies there is a story, in this case of a local miller called Old John who was killed during a bonfire which was held on the spot, with the sham tower being raised to his memory. Another local story I heard, though, was that the arch to the side was later added to make it look like a beer mug!*

Bastle Houses

In the more troublesome border regions of the North of England, Scottish raids were still a problem in the 16th and 17th centuries, so farmers developed a two-storey form of defensible house called a 'bastle'. These rectangular stone buildings had ground floor accommodation for the livestock with a door in one of the end walls, while above was the living area accessed by a retractable ladder from a door in the side wall (a permanent stone staircase was often added later). Today these houses either stand as ruins within fields, are used as barns, or remain within a later farm.

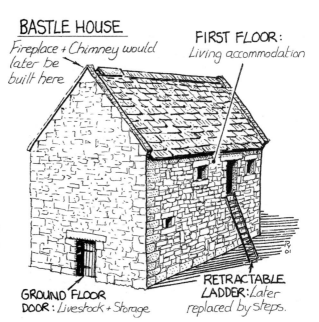

BASTLE HOUSE
Fireplace + Chimney would later be built here

FIRST FLOOR: Living accommodation

RETRACTABLE LADDER: Later replaced by steps.

GROUND FLOOR DOOR: Livestock + Storage

■ FIG 4.11: A drawing of a bastle house in an original form showing some of its typical features.

The Church

The religious changes depending on which monarch was on the throne must have had a bewildering effect on the local parish church during the 16th and 17th centuries. It was not until after the Restoration of Charles II in 1660 that the interior of the building finally settled down to a form which we would be more familiar with today. By then the colourful and mysterious medieval Catholic church had been destroyed. Icons, shrines, altars, and roods had been removed, stained glass windows had been smashed and replaced with clear glass, and wall paintings were whitewashed over. The church must have suddenly appeared bright and pure. No longer would mass be chanted in Latin from behind screens, now the priests would turn, face the congregation and preach in English from newly constructed pulpits. The altar was replaced by a communion table while a royal coat of arms appeared above the chancel arch.

In some circumstances parts of the medieval church were saved from destruction, especially in the more remote regions of the country. Other features like the wall paintings have since been uncovered and saved while stained glass, which was often left shattered on the ground outside the church, was collected together and reinserted - usually into somewhat abstract patterns - by Victorian and later restorers (see Fig 3.27 - page 100).

119

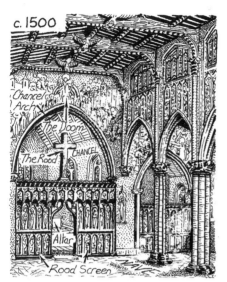 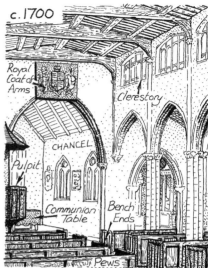

■ *FIG 4.12: Two drawings of the inside of a church, the left hand one showing features of the medieval building with painted walls and the rood screen while the right hand one shows it two hundred years later with whitewashed walls and seating.*

The fabric of the church itself changed little in this period, although there may have been some partial rebuilding or embellishment during the 18th century in a classic style, to fit in with a lord's landscaped park. Any new churches tended to be associated with these garden schemes or in towns although a new tower or reconstructed body of the church when the previous part was unsafe is quite common. Inside the congregation may have lost their colourful paintings but at least they now had seating. In the medieval period fixed seats were not practical as the church was also used for secular events, but once these took place elsewhere, and there were more funds available, wooden pews appeared such that by the 17th century most churches had them. These could have highly decorated bench ends, one of the few examples of medieval art which often survives today. By the 18th century more private and comfortable box pews appeared which were entered through a door, while within the nave and aisles a gallery could be inserted. Both of these were used as private family seating for the local squire, although the latter feature appeared in many town churches to increase the capacity in the face of a booming population.

■ *FIG 4.13: WEST WYCOMBE, BUCKS: This medieval parish church had a dramatic make-over in the 1750s and 60s when the local lord rebuilt the nave and tower in Classic style. Note that the chancel nearest to us is still in its Gothic form. Meetings of the notorious Hell Fire Club were said to have taken place within the golden ball on top of the tower!*

The Churchyard and Monuments

Outside the church there were equally dramatic changes as the old medieval stone cross which stood over the graveyard was also destroyed. The stumps of these can still be found sometimes with later replacement crosses fitted back on top. In the 17th century the first gravestones were erected to mark individual burials so the churchyard started to take the form we are familiar with today.

Tombs, wall tablets and monuments for the wealthy and important in the parish were still to be found inside the church. Separate family chapels or side aisles survived the Reformation although they lost their altars, and in the following centuries they became even more popular. The size and grandeur of monuments in these private chapels or in the main body of the church increased and by the end of the 17th century they could be huge, ostentatious set pieces which overpowered the modest surroundings of the building. They followed the architectural fashions of the day from the Renaissance to the Classics and were made from a variety of materials until after the Restoration when marble was almost exclusively used. The people and dates on these monuments may be of some help in tracing the history of influential people in your village, while the scale and opulence of the piece may give you a clue to the person's aspirations, wealth or popularity.

The Parish

Partly due to social and economic changes but also because of the void left by the dissolved monasteries, hospitals and chantries, the role of the parish was to change in this period, as it was chosen to take on secular duties in addition to its ecclesiastic ones. From 1538 each parish had to record the births, marriages and burials in a register, in 1555 the Highways Act made it responsible for the maintenance of roads, while the 1601 Poor Law Act put the raising and distribution of poor relief in its hands. New, unpaid officials were elected from the parish to administer these duties, including a constable who would report regularly on matters of crime and disorder, and the churchwarden who had to keep an eye on the body of the church and the minds of the parishioners. In addition to this the collection of local, county and national taxes fell upon their shoulders. The records which these bodies had to keep, like the Parish Register, have become vital sources of information about villages up to the 19th century.

Nonconformist Chapels

The Church of England's attempts to tolerate all the various factions within it were to be partly responsible for the Civil War, and upon the Restoration of the Monarchy in 1660 those groups who would not conform to the Anglican doctrine were legally excluded. These nonconformists were in 1689 permitted to worship and in the next ten years nearly 3,000 Quaker, Baptist, Congregationalist and Unitarian chapels appeared. These and many other groups found popularity mainly in the new towns and fledgling industrial villages where the Church of England was slow to erect new buildings, so that by the 19th century nearly half of the church-attending public went to chapel.

■ *FIG 4.14: CHENIES, BUCKS: The front of a Baptist chapel dating from 1799 with a typical three bay symmetrical frontage and arched windows (the porch was added later).*

Most villages will still have at least one chapel, although many today have been converted to residential or other uses. The earliest were humble meeting houses but by the late 18th century more impressive chapels with symmetrical classical and later Gothic fronts are to be found. In many of these new villages in the industrial areas the appearance of a chapel was the first part of unifying the various workers and their families into a community.

The Rectory or Vicarage

The position of the clergy in the village community was elevated through this period, as the local rector or vicar became better educated, more often than not married with a family, and benefited from the increased tithes due to agricultural improvements (a vicar was the incumbent of a parish where the tithes formerly were taken by a religious house or lord, while a rector was called such where the tithes had formerly been kept by the local priest). By the late 18th century he would now find himself on the same social standing as the lesser gentry, and was one of the most important figures in the village beside the squire, even though the influence of the Church of England was waning due to the nonconformists and the new understanding of science. The early rectory and vicarage complexes would have included outbuildings as the clergyman would have also farmed his glebeland, while the familiar large houses which are often only second in size to the manor house tend to appear in the 18th century.

Castles

By the 16th century those castles which had survived the Middle Ages were in the main residential with larger windows fitted with glass and additional buildings added to suit their non defensive role. Other ones may have been retained for other roles, especially in the towns, but the majority were either ruined or had already been removed. There was, however, an Indian summer for many English castles in the Civil War, when they were refortified during the conflict. Unfortunately the important military role they played led Cromwell and his army to render them unusable once the war was won, so much so that on many sites today only their earthworks remain.

Other types of temporary fortifications were raised during the Civil War and the remains of many can be found around villages today. Documentation, maps and records from this time may help identify and confirm the origins of these earthworks and perhaps even relate them to one of the many minor skirmishes which occurred across the country.

Military Establishments

The feudal system had always supplied the medieval king with knights and hordes of untrained peasants to fight his battles, although mercenaries had also been used. The first professional fighting force was probably Cromwell's New Model Army which played its part in turning round the fortunes of the Parliamentarians in the Civil War. By the 18th century our numerous conflicts with European states were being fought on land and sea by a huge and partly professional force many times larger than any previous English army.

To support this, training schools, military ranges and barracks were built while naval dockyards were either constructed or existing ones expanded, all of this inevitably creating extra demand for produce and employment which would have affected surrounding villages.

Mills

During this period there were many changes to mills in both their form and use. Water wheels, which had previously turned the millstones which ground the grain, were now increasingly powering machinery. Fulling, hammer, paper and cotton mills appeared all over the country by the end of the 18th century. No longer were they humble, timber structures but now large industrial buildings which would be a vital source of employment if sited in a village. Some were also built to pump out mines although these were among the first to be replaced by steam engines.

Windmills also developed in their structural form. There was still the old post mill design based on a central post around which the whole building would have to be turned, firstly by hand and then later by a tail, in order to face into the wind. The tail was a separate fan on the end of a long rail. When the wind changed direction, it turned the fan which in turn rotated the windmill to reface the wind. The wooden sails you see today are only the frames which supported the actual material sails which would have been drawn across them when in use. The smock mill (with a timber-clad exterior) and the tower mill (usually a conical brick structure) improved on this by having the sails and tail fixed to a cap which rotated separately from the building. Those which stand today date mainly from the 18th and 19th centuries, though there are a couple of 17th century post mills which have been restored.

Farm Buildings

By 1800 most of the building types which we would now expect to see in a farmyard had appeared. The barns were usually smaller versions of the tithe barns described in Chapter 2, while the grain which resulted from the threshing was stored in a granary. These could be small, timber-framed buildings set on mushroom shaped stones or a room above a cart shed, in both cases raised off the ground to keep rodents away from the grain. Other buildings which made up the farmstead could include animal sheds and pens, stables, a dairy and the farmhouse itself.

■ FIG 4.15: WEALD AND DOWNLAND OPEN AIR MUSEUM: A barn dating from around 1700 with the two great doors opening up onto the threshing floor where the crop held in one half was battered to separate the grain and stalk while the husks blew away in the wind.

■ FIG 4.16: WEALD AND DOWNLAND OPEN AIR MUSEUM: A timber-framed granary raised upon distinctive mushroom shaped stones to prevent rodents getting at the grain stored within.

Inns, Taverns and Alehouses

The increase in road travel through the 17th and 18th centuries made this the boom time for roadside inns and taverns. Those villages which straddled a main road, especially a turnpike road, would see new or rebuilt inns with archways for coaches and horses to pass under to reach the stables in the rear courtyard. They would often be imposing two or three-storey buildings offering food, drink and lodgings with sometimes huge signs hanging off elaborate metal brackets outside.

The humble pub that we are familiar with did not develop until the 19th century. Beer was still brewed and consumed at home, though the village taverns or alehouses, often just a single room run by a spinster, were becoming the social hub of the working community.

Houses

This is the period when most of the oldest timber-framed, brick, cob and stone houses in our villages were built. We should rightly admire their quality for they have survived hundreds of years, but should remember that even the most humble of these were built for the wealthier members of the community. The majority of the workers in the village lived in single or two-roomed cottages, hovels and longhouses, most of which have long since collapsed.

Those who benefited from the increased prosperity from the mid 16th century built themselves new houses. The period from 1570 to 1640 was named the 'Great Rebuilding' by the historian W.G. Hoskins who first recognised this development in the South of England, and in the North during the 18th century. These range from the new mansions and houses of the gentry to the more modest homes of yeoman and tenant farmers. Later concentrated periods of building in your village may relate to a prosperous period in its history, a successful local industry, the enclosure of your parish or the rebuilding of an estate.

There was even in the rural parts of the country a certain aspiration to keep up with the latest fashions in house building, which started usually with the manor or mansion but later filtered down to the lesser houses. In general the materials used were still vernacular as only the wealthy could afford to transport stone from outside the locality, although finely cut pieces of masonry were pilfered from the old monasteries and abandoned churches. Timber-framed houses were constructed well into the 18th century especially at the lowest end of the scale, but brick, locally produced in the new brickworks, started to gain favour. Bricks

■ *FIG 4.17: WEALD AND DOWNLAND OPEN AIR MUSEUM: A labourer's cottage dating from the 17th century. Note the fencing made from woven coppiced branches and the garden laid out with vegetable plots and fruit trees.*

were also used on corners and in horizontal bands on houses built with flints and pebbles. In the 18th century bricks were covered in stucco or cement which was then patterned to imitate masonry, a surprisingly common occurrence in many a grand 18th century house! In areas where stone could be readily quarried this continued as the main building material, while in certain parts like Devon, Dorset, Buckinghamshire and East Anglia a variety of methods of using clays and muds interlaced with straw, sand and stone were popular up until the 19th century.

If you could not afford to build a new one you could always reface your out of date or poor quality timber-framed house by giving it a new facade. This could be done by coating plaster over strips of wood fixed to the front of the house, and then combing patterns into it. This process, called pargeting, was especially popular in East Anglia in the late 17th century, although most examples you see today are more recent. Again in East Anglia and also later in the South East horizontal wooden boards were used as a weatherproof cover while in the late 18th century Mathematical tiles could be hung on the outside to imitate brickwork (which also had the advantage of avoiding the brick tax from 1784-1850). By this time it was also common for cements to be applied onto the front of the house to cover rough stone, poor timber and common brick and to give classic proportions to the rickety building. These refaced houses can be identified today by looking firstly for an uneven level of windows, secondly for an exposed

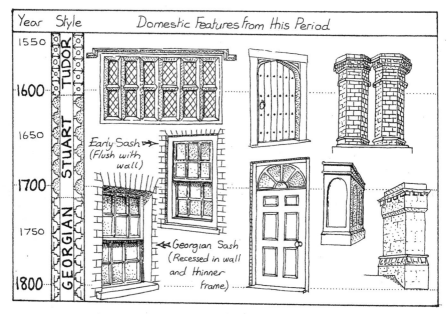

■ FIG 4.18: A chart showing some of the architectural features which can be found on the important houses in a village, the style to which they belong and their approximate date.

timber-frame down the side and rear, and thirdly by the interior which will have retained the low, exposed timber ceiling of the original house (see Fig 4.31 - page 140).

The regional and period variations in architectural design are too great to be included in detail here (see Chapter 6 for a list of books which cover this subject). Generally across the lowland regions single pile houses (1 room deep) with two to four rooms in a variety of arrangement was usual for the average villager, while larger houses were double piled (2 rooms deep) with perhaps a third storey, attic rooms or a cellar. In the upland regions the same proportions could be found but longhouses of the medieval type were still popular as were a larger type known as 'laithe houses' where the whole was still under one roof but the agricultural end was a separate barn rather than an interconnected byre.

Almshouses and Schools

After the Reformation the building of almshouses to accommodate the old and infirm of the village became the social responsibility of the lord and parishioners. Many villages still retain these distinctive buildings which can date from the late

■ *FIG 4.19: MAPLEDURHAM, OXON: A row of single storey almshouses dating from the early 17th century.*

15th up to the 19th century. They are most commonly a long row of single-storey cottages in a unifying architectural style, usually still with matching doors and windows. Later ones may have a symmetrical frontage with a central raised feature, while some larger types were built in a U shape or even a fully enclosed quadrangle with a separate chapel or adjacent to a church.

Schools were not compulsory in villages until the Education Acts in the late 19th century. The wealthy members of the community appreciated the long term benefits of a good education and would have sent their offspring off to schools and colleges in the towns and cities. By the 18th century though, half the children of Village England had some form of schooling, but only in basic Mathematics and English, and then it would have been interrupted by the seasonal demands of agriculture. Local benefactors did build some schools in villages, but they may not necessarily have been welcoming to all members of the community. As with the almshouses a plaque or tablet will usually be on display at the front to name the founder and the date of construction.

Pounds, Lockups and Stocks

The parish constable (not a policeman in the modern sense but a local worker with the additional duty of reporting on crime and disorder) would have had a lockup to hold suspects, which could have been a small single cell square or round building or just part of an existing structure.

Everyone is familiar with the scene of a man with head and arms dangling from a set of stocks while villagers throw rotten vegetables at him. These were used for justice from the 13th to the 19th century, although those which do survive, often preserved on the village green, are probably later ones.

You are more likely to find a pound in your village today than the above. These were built to hold stray livestock, and therefore died out when the parish fields were enclosed. Those which survive are built of brick or stone though many may have originally been just a fenced enclosure.

Roads and Canals

The increase in long distance travel by officials, merchants and the gentry, as well as the transporting of goods and livestock, led to demands for improvement to the roads. Although the parish became responsible for their maintenance in the 16th century, their physical condition did not dramatically improve until the forming of Turnpike Trusts more than a hundred years later. A group of local landlords would form a trust, then obtain authority from Parliament to take over and improve a stretch of perhaps ten miles of road. Their improvements may have even stretched to diverting the road or constructing a new route up a hill, both of which could have by-passed a village, directly affecting its prosperity or as previously stated causing it to migrate towards the new road.

When completed the Turnpike Trust would set up gates and toll houses and collect a fee from travellers for using the road, the money being split between future maintenance and profit for the investors. The word 'turnpike' comes from the spikes or 'pikes' which were fitted along the top of the 'turning' gates to stop horsemen jumping over them. Round and hexagonal toll houses are still a common sight in villages and along roads, and most date to the boom in these road improvements from the mid to late 18th century. Milestones carved with destinations and mileages are another notable feature which can be found along old turnpike roads, and are marked by an 'MS' on Ordnance Survey maps.

Droving cattle and sheep from the upland areas to the main cities, especially London, became important from the mid 17th until the 19th century. The driving

■ *FIG 4.20: DORCHESTER, OXON: A typical brick toll house dating from the early 19th century on the old London to Gloucester turnpike road.*

of livestock was a planned project by licensed drovers and they kept to special routes which were preferably away from turnpike tolls and built up areas. Ideally they would have grazing areas along the way and inns or farms, where there was a field or stance for the livestock to be impounded overnight and accommodation for the men. The railways ended the droving trade though the remains of routes, especially in the uplands, and the overnight stances - identifiable by names like 'Halfpenny' or 'Broad Field' - can still be traced today as well as the inns and farms used (the name Halfpenny coming from the fee charged for an overnight stay).

The quantity and size of goods which a horse and cart could pull was limited even where the roads were good. River travel was an answer and from the 17th century improvements were put in place to make transportation easier although flooding and droughts were still problems. This form of travel though was no use if your quarry, mine or factory was nowhere near a suitable river, or if you wanted to move goods across the country. The answer was to build canals. During the last half of the 18th and early 19th century thousands of miles of waterways were created, linking industrial and agricultural areas with towns and cities. Unfortunately the long term commercial viability of the canals was limited by the dimensions of narrow locks (approximately 72 ft x 7 ft 6 ins), which therefore restricted the size of boat and more importantly the load it could carry. Although later ones were built wider the restriction of the narrow locks somewhere along the journey affected the cost and speed of transporting goods to the extent that the majority of canals closed in the face of competition from the railways and roads.

This commercial shortcoming has meant that the original narrow canals and their Georgian and Regency buildings were never replaced and are distinctive features of many villages today. The canal could have affected the settlement around it in a number of ways, for instance from the benefits of an increase in trade now they could transport agricultural produce and industrial goods cheaply and for greater distances. Also from the building of wharfs, boatyards and inns, especially around canal junctions and flights of locks, which gave employment and as with the main roads of the day drew housing towards them. Your village may have been just a hamlet off the beaten track before the canal transformed it into a bustling centre only for the subsequent decline of the waterway to return it to obscurity. Just because a canal is not visible today does not mean there is not a disused one which was filled in; or perhaps one was surveyed and planned but never actually built. The documents and maps from these lost or failed projects may survive and along with the records of existing canals can play a vital part in tracing the history of your village.

■ FIG 4.21: HAWKESBURY JUNCTION, COVENTRY: A settlement built around a junction on the Coventry Canal with cast iron bridges, a stop lock and a pumping house with the chimney for its steam engine.

The Villagers

In this period there is a clearer and widening gap between the various classes in the country. It would be wrong to assume that the close knit community, working for each other, is a situation which has always existed in your village. With the end of the feudal system the landowners who previously had contact with members of the community through the organising of the agricultural calendar, now through either leasing off their land or enclosure had no need to communicate with the majority of the villagers.

At the top of this social order would have been a member of the gentry. These ranged from dukes, lords and baronets, who increasingly were those who had climbed in rank rather than members of the old aristocratic families who had inherited their titles, down to the lesser gentlemen and squires. Their standing would have been judged mainly on the quantity of land they owned, but to an increasing amount on their education. Many 18th century gentlemen spent their early years abroad on grand tours which took in Paris and Italy, to study the classic art and architecture and more often than not bring half of it back with them! This background manifests itself in the landscape parks and classical mansions they built.

Those in a position of wealth also had more time for leisure, two of the favourite pastimes being horse racing and hunting. It may be surprising to find that there were many racecourses laid out around the countryside in the 17th and 18th centuries, for instance on the now sacred lands at Port Meadow in Oxford and Runnymede in Surrey! Most of these have gone but their presence may be preserved on old maps or in field names. Hunting has been the favourite pastime of lords ever since the Saxon times, but its current form of men dressed in scarlet jackets and black velvet caps chasing the wily fox developed in the Georgian period. Deer was the favourite quarry of medieval kings and lords but with a decline in the parks and woodland, the hare and then after the Restoration in 1660 the fox, which had previously been regarded as an inferior target, became popular.

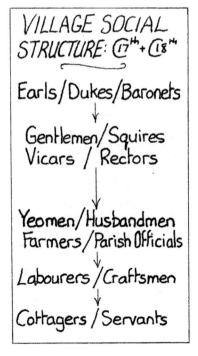

VILLAGE SOCIAL STRUCTURE: 17th + 18th

Earls / Dukes / Baronets
↓
Gentlemen / Squires
Vicars / Rectors
↓
Yeomen / Husbandmen
Farmers / Parish Officials
↓
Labourers / Craftsmen
↓
Cottagers / Servants

There are many features associated with fox hunting which you can recognise around your village, for instance stables and kennels to keep the hounds and horses, fox coverts (often named as such on maps) or artificial earths which were created to encourage them to breed. Around the famous hunting county of Leicestershire there are still special field hedges of thorn bushes with rails on one or both sides, designed in the 18th century, for horses to jump. In the Lake District the tradition is to hunt with special packs of hounds over the fells while the huntsmen follow them on foot.

Further down the social order were the lesser landowners or freeholders who in addition to managing their farms would also fill the positions of the various parish officials. In areas affected by enclosure though, some would find it hard to pay for new buildings, hedging, fencing and legal expenses, so they might sell up and became tenants or use their capital to move into other fields. Generally this yeoman class diminishes from the 17th century and the farmer, renting a new enclosed farm from the squire, becomes dominant in the middle order of the village.

At the bottom of the pile were the cottagers, landless labourers and domestic servants who by the 18th century made up half of the population of England. Despite the improving living conditions and levels of education for some, this group still lived in primitive accommodation, were widely superstitious, were more influenced by folklore than the word of the vicar and on the whole were illiterate. Many men would be employed on a seasonal basis at the local hiring fairs, while the women and children would gain additional funds from grazing livestock, domestic work, or a local craft and industry.

The parish poor rates introduced in 1601 were designed to help those of this class unable to support themselves, but as their numbers multiplied through this period there were various alterations to the system. The Act of Settlement of 1662 tied a person's relief to the village of their birth; workhouses were set up from 1695 onwards where the poor could work for their living (though they rarely did); while the later Speenhamland System of 1795 tied the amount paid to the price of a loaf of bread. As previously explained, the enclosures deprived these villagers of land for grazing, and those which had not left due to this were to find it even harder to make ends meet in the next period as industrialisation killed off the cottage industries they now relied on.

SUMMARY

The farmer contemplating his smart new farmyard, house and fields in 1800 would be looking forward to a prosperous future, while some of those working his lands were scraping around for a living. The village was no longer the centre of an agricultural system, but a home for those who provided services for it. In the final period up to the modern day these services would become fused into the trades and their specialised buildings which we associate with the traditional village, only for the social and economic changes of the 20th century to kill them off.

STILL THERE
FEATURES TO LOOK OUT FOR

■ *FIG 4.22: BRILL, BUCKS: A post mill dating from the late 17th century. The ground to the right of the mill was excavated for the local brick, tile and pottery industry which dates from the 14th to the 20th century.*

■ *FIG 4.23: TISSINGTON, DERBYSHIRE: A Georgian gravestone dating from 1732.*

■ FIG 4.24: SHARDLOES, BUCKS: A lodge house, one of a matching pair which flank the entrance gate to the late 18th century house.

■ FIG 4.25: CULHAM, OXON: A set of stocks on the green at Culham.

■ *FIG 4.26: MAPLEDURHAM, OXON: This old mill, the last working one on the Thames, dates from the 16th century although most of what you see is from later periods.*

■ *FIG 4.27: DOVECOTE, near WORCESTER: A rather grand dovecote which probably dates from the early 17th century. This form of timber-framing, known as 'close studding', was popular in the 16th and 17th centuries and was something of a status symbol, which also shows how important the keeping of pigeons was.*

■ *FIG 4.28: DORCHESTER, OXON: A milestone alongside the London to Gloucester turnpike road.*

■ *FIG 4.29: LACEY GREEN, BUCKS: A smock mill which dates in part from the 17th century. Only the triangular top section would turn to face the direction of the wind, with the lower weatherboarded smock remaining stationary.*

■ *FIG 4.30: ARDLEY, OXON: An enclosure road with its distinctive wide verges and hawthorn hedges.*

■ *FIG 4.31: MIDHURST, WEST SUSSEX: An example of a timber-framed building where, in order to make it more fashionable, a classic frontage has been added facing the street.*

■ *FIG 4.32: TISSINGTON, DERBYSHIRE: A 17th century memorial to the Fitzherbert family which shows the grandeur of monuments which can be found in even the most humble of parish churches.*

■ *FIG 4.33: CHELMORTON, DERBYSHIRE: The walls which were built when this parish was enclosed follow the old strips of the open fields. The village runs right to left through the middle of the picture with the fields running at right angles from behind the houses, in such a regulated manner as to suggest that this village was planned in the medieval period.*

■ FIG 4.34: LAXTON, NOTTS: This unique village is still surrounded by working open fields with the farms still lining the main road through the village, like this 18th century example with the date 1760 in the end gable of the nearest building.

■ FIG 4.35: WHEATLEY, OXON: An old lock-up known as The Round House despite its hexagonal plan, which was built in 1834.

■ *FIG 4.36: ABBOT'S BROMLEY, STAFFS: From the later Middle Ages, many markets gained a covered area which could range from a simple structure like this butter cross, up to market houses with two storeys.*

■ *FIG 4.37: THE CLAYDONS, BUCKS: This view shows the typically symmetrical classic frontage of the West Wing of Claydon House which was built in the 1750s.*

■ *FIG 4.38: DENHAM, BUCKS: Although only a minor today, this village road was probably on a major coach route judging by the two pubs at the end and the archway on what was most likely a coaching inn. Many dead end roads or quiet lanes may have been busy routes in the past around which your village developed. The traffic was later lost perhaps when the road was rebuilt avoiding the village which even happened as long ago as the 18th century.*

■ *FIG 4.39: THE PEAK DISTRICT: A landscape boxed into tidy parcels by the enclosure acts. This scene of straight dry stone walls laid out in the 18th and 19th centuries is repeated all over the upland regions of England.*

CHAPTER 5
INDUSTRY AND SUBURBIA

The Victorian and Modern Age: 1800 - 2000

■ *FIG 5.1: Our imaginary village has now completed its journey up to the present day. The mansion house on the hill in the distance is now a business centre, but before its lord sold the estate he established tree plantations over much of it in an attempt to increase its income. To the right, below the hill, the small settlement which was growing around the mill has now, with the arrival of the railway in addition to the canal and river, developed into an industrious village, leaving its original core isolated in the foreground. The church has been restored with exposed stonework and Gothic details, while the manor house to its side is now a private house hidden behind trees and electric gates. Although at first glance the changes here are not as drastic as in previous periods, if you look closely you can see evidence of the huge improvements to the standard of living for the villagers. Mains water, drainage and sewerage have brought hygiene and convenience, while electricity powers heating and appliances. Tarmac roads, pavements and street lights permit travel all year round and the telephone and post box are signs of communication with a wider, outside world.*

Although there have been some new arrivals in our picture, unlike previous periods there has been a large element of preservation and retention. This seemingly timeless packaging though disguises the underlying changes to the village's contents which have come about since 1800. This chapter will describe some of the events and the social and physical alterations which occurred as a result and are still today changing the role of the English village.

THE NATIONAL PICTURE

The opening of the 19th century found Britain at war with Napoleon. Hostilities with France lasted intermittently from 1793 to 1815 and there were numerous effects upon the nation apart from the threat of invasion. Agriculture had to respond to the blockades and production and wages rose, while our Army grew from 40,000 to 500,000 including conscripts, volunteers and part timers. Unfortunately at the end of the conflict thousands of soldiers and sailors flooded the job market, so that wages fell and agricultural labourers rioted and threatened revolution.

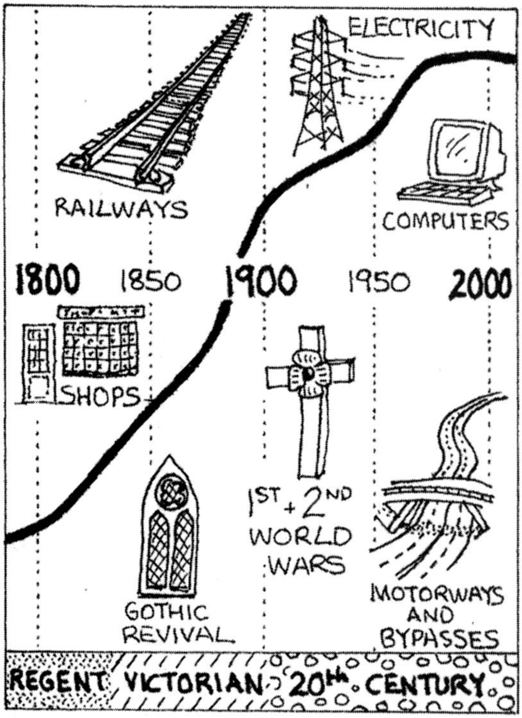

■ *FIG 5.2: The final length of the population line shows the rapid rise of the past two hundred years especially in the 19th century and post war period.*

146

The French Revolution struck fear into the aristocracy at home and they acted promptly to ward off any threat to their position of power. The Peterloo Massacre, the Tolpuddle Martyrs and the Swing Riots are examples of this discontent which ended with deportation and death for some of the participants. The reforms of the 1830s, especially that of Parliament in 1832, probably saved England from spiralling into the revolutionary fever which had spread across mainland Europe.

The rising population due to a decreasing death rate, earlier marriages and a higher number of births played its part in fuelling what has been described by 20th century historians as the Industrial Revolution. These increasing numbers though lived in the cities but as their conditions and working hours improved they had more time and money for leisure. Firstly the middle classes at the turn of the 20th century, and then the working classes in the 1930s began the invasion of the countryside, inspired by romantic images of timeless, rustic villages from poetry and paintings of the day.

Members of some rural communities had been involved in the Crimea and then the Boer War now that the Army comprised volunteer soldiers, but virtually no village escaped the massacre of the First World War. Memorial crosses record the numerous young men who lost their lives, crippling a whole generation from labourers to young aristocrats. The loss of these male heirs, the agricultural depression and the fixing of rents in the war resulted in a great sell off of many aristocratic estates especially in the 1920s.

The loss of these estates, the decline of the mining industry and then the mechanisation of agriculture especially after the Second World War has seen the numbers of those who work on the land decline, in some cases leading to abandonment of settlements even into modern times. Offsetting this are the incomers from the towns and cities seeking their rural idyll away from the noise and pollution of the urban environment. Since the forming of County Councils in 1888 the village has also fitted increasingly into a larger picture, influenced by decisions taken at County Hall, Westminster and Brussels more than those made in the local manor or parish.

AGRICULTURE

The enclosure movement described in the previous chapter continued up until the middle of the 19th century, creating a network of new, efficient farms linked into an increasingly world wide market. This system had been tested during the Napoleonic Wars when agriculture had to feed a nation deprived of imported food by the blockades of foreign ports. The artificially high prices which resulted

■ *FIG 5.3: This chart shows the dramatic turnaround in the 19th century between those living in the countryside and those living in towns and cities with a population greater than 5,000. You can see the rapid rise in urban numbers and the steady performance of the smaller towns and villages, but the significant reduction in the proportion of the population working the land.*

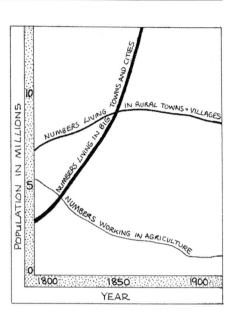

were maintained after the war by the Corn Law Act of 1815 which was designed to protect the income of the landowners by imposing duties on imported grain, ruling out cheaper competition from abroad. The poor suffered as a result from the high price of bread, an excess of labour and the effects of enclosure, such that the exodus to the cities increased. Although farming was still labour intensive, the total numbers working the land fell.

The repeal of the Corn Laws in 1846, as a result of the suffering in Ireland from the potato famine, did not flood the market with the cheap imports that the landowners and farmers feared, instead they entered a period referred to as the Golden Age of High Farming. Around villages all over the country Victorian brick and stone farmsteads record this time of prosperity, with new buildings for livestock, grain storage and farm machinery set around a central courtyard. The problem was that the industry was still looking in upon itself and did not foresee the threat coming from abroad. It arrived in the 1870s when huge quantities of grain from America and Canada flooded onto the market and from 1879 the price of corn fell. New advances in refrigeration also affected the livestock producers as cheaper meat could now be imported from as far away as New Zealand.

The resulting agricultural depression was to last into the early 1900s and had great long term effects on village life. There was a continuing decline in numbers working the fields, especially from the younger generation many of whom left agriculture for new careers at home or in the cities, while the reduction of rents reduced incomes to the owners of the estates. The decline and decay which set in was recorded in paintings and photographs, creating an image of charming, rusticated villages which in part triggered the love affair the urban classes were to have with rural life throughout the 20th century. What would have been the reaction had the pictures been taken in prosperous times when the buildings were new, steam powered the farm machinery and noisy railways moved masses of livestock and grain?

Not everyone saw decline in this period of general economic gloom. The rapidly increasing urban population benefited from higher wages and could afford a more diverse diet. The working classes wanted meat while the middle classes sought fruit and vegetables. Those farmers who could adapt turned their land over to market gardening, greenhouses, orchards and pasture to satisfy this demand. In other areas of the country the old systems of farming had been little affected by the changes to the English lowlands. On the uplands, sheep and cattle farming continued as it had done for millennia, still structured around the family unit and small hamlets. The only intrusion of technology here was the railway which opened up new markets to them and encouraged the taking in of more land up in the hills. Other regions specialised, the most notable perhaps being Kent where hops were grown, dried in the distinctive oast houses and then sold for beer production.

Agriculture during and since the 20th century has been shaped by the belief, born out of the World Wars, that Britain should be able to feed itself. In the early 1900s we imported more grain than we produced ourselves and starvation was only avoided in wartime by the efforts of the farming industry to increase output. The subsidies offered by central government since have encouraged farmers to plough more land, use pesticides and grub out hedges to make larger fields more suitable for the new tractors and machines which they could now afford to buy. Unfortunately these new farming methods have further reduced the need for agricultural labourers and could result in damage to the flora and fauna in the surrounding countryside.

Two hundred years ago the vast majority of villagers worked the land, while today the farmhands who survive are more likely to be outnumbered by commuters, businessmen and the retired. Agriculture has shaped the countryside since the first Neolithic farmers 6,000 years ago but now the rural economy is influenced more by tourism and leisure, and it is the fortune of these industries which now has the greater effect on most villages.

Woodland

Much of the woodland today is or was planted for commercial reasons. Industries like ship building, tanning, iron and furniture maintained either coppice for fuel or larger trees for timber depending on their requirements and the economic situation. For villagers the woodland continued as it had done for centuries to be a source of fuel and building material, while gamekeepers protected it for wildfowl and fox coverts.

In the 20th century the decline of grazing on those commons and wastes which survived the enclosure movement permitted a secondary growth of trees to become established as there were no animals to eat the young shoots. Disused industrial and military land can also in an amazingly short time become scrub and then develop into woodland. The humps and bumps which you probably would not think twice about in a wood today can be worth investigating as when cross referenced to old maps and photos can reveal a surprisingly recent yet forgotten landscape.

The greatest threat to woodland came from agriculture in the boom years of the mid 19th century and since the Second World War, with the grubbing up of trees and hedges to increase arable land. The commercial planting of conifers and the tinkering around with existing woods by introducing unsuitable new species has also had a long term negative effect. The ruining of the soil which results can leave open moorland once the new trees are felled, while some of these fashionable species, especially sycamore and rhododendrons, have become pests.

NATIONAL PARKS

The introduction after the last war of National Parks and the growth of conservation bodies like the National Trust has led to great swathes of the countryside coming under the influence of in effect new landlords. Villages which fall into these areas have been protected and preserved with restrictions sometimes not just limiting building but also maintaining the numbers who work in local industry, crafts and farming.

THE VILLAGE

The development or decline of your village in the 19th and 20th centuries depended on a number of factors: the success of farms and local industries and their ability to adapt to a rapidly changing market, the presence of a railway and latterly A roads and motorways, the close proximity of a town and city and the benevolent actions of landlords, government and other groups. Some maintained

■ *FIG 5.4: OLD WARDEN, BEDS: A picturesque cottage in this 19th century estate village where not only did the local lord have these rustic houses constructed but he also insisted that the inhabitants dressed up in tall hats and red cloaks to complete the effect.*

population levels or even grew due to the above factors while some even as late as the mid 20th century declined and were in exceptional circumstances deserted because they were not in such a fortunate position.

It was recognised in the 19th century that another limitation on the development of a settlement and the form it would take was whether it was 'open' or 'closed' or a mix of both. If the village was dominated by a resident squire or an interested but absent lord who probably owned the majority of the land, then he could control it and close its doors to undesirables (hence 'closed village'). The physical signs would be a neat, planned layout, a number of large farms, housing of a good quality but limited availability and probably only one pub and shop. Although the villagers may have benefited from low rent, they would have had to do as the lord wished, and that could include influence on their religious practices and political leanings.

In contrast, an open village was one without these controls where there were numerous smallholders, a large proportion of peasant families and local industries. These would be unplanned settlements with poorer housing, a large number of pubs and shops, and nonconformist chapels. The villagers would pay rent but had freedom in matters of managing their plots and their personal beliefs. It is in these open villages that you are more likely to see a population growth in the 19th century.

With the breaking up and selling off of estates in the 20th century, villages have been more open to new development. Those within the commuter belts have seen housing filling in vacant plots or lands around the edges of the settlement while villages in attractive settings have drawn people looking for a retirement or second home. Old cottages have been renovated and extended, barns converted and even chapels fitted out with domestic trappings. New town developments to house people from the major cities after the Second World War have swallowed up villages and farmland although the creeping mass of suburbia which threatened to run out of control has been restricted by designated green belts.

Model Villages

Many villages either completely or partially owe their existence to the actions, benevolence or whims of their landlord. A distinctive type from the 19th century are the villages established by factory owners to house their workers, ranging from highly decorative pieces of architecture to more functional industrial villages.

■ *FIG 5.5: STEWARTBY, BEDS: A complete village started in the late 1920s to house workers from the adjacent brickworks, complete with green, shop, school and community hall and named after the chairman of the company, Mr H. Stewart.*

Some places benefited from the actions of philanthropists who improved housing and living conditions, again usually to some architectural plan which could include new churches, schools and reading rooms. There are also villages specifically created by either existing or incoming religious groups. Although not 'model villages', the actions of Government-backed schemes like the Land Settlement Association rejuvenated existing villages and changed their physical appearance to suit the incoming beneficiaries.

Fishing Villages

The first fishing villages were probably seasonal settlements associated with the main village of the parish further inland. Those who worked the land during spring and summer could spend the winter months fishing, although as transport was limited their catch could only be consumed locally. Most inland manors had fish ponds and course rather than sea fish were consumed. By the 15th century some of our oldest fishing villages had become established, but it was not until the coming of the railways and developments in refrigeration in the 19th century that most took their present shape and size.

Military Villages

The effect of an increasingly large and diverse military force in the 19th and 20th centuries led directly to the founding and expanding of settlements. Army, Navy and Airforce camps have engulfed old hamlets, estates or virgin sites creating a modern village with regimented rows of barracks and family homes, shops, churches and social facilities. Associated with these are shooting ranges, storage depots, roads and railways and airfields particularly in the south and east of England.

Desertion and Destruction

Despite the cases of new and expanded villages for military, industrial and urban demands, these same pressures have led to the removal or abandonment of others even in recent times. A number of Second World War airfields were built on top of settlements, while the MOD cleared hamlets and farms in creating army camps. The urban demand for water forced councils to build reservoirs, flood valleys and cause the destruction of settlements including villages. Numerous declining industrial or agricultural villages were finally abandoned in the 20th century when councils refused to make up roads or provide services, forcing the remaining inhabitants to move into new towns while their old homes were either left to ruin or were bulldozed.

■ *FIG 5.6: MARDALE GREEN, LAKE DISTRICT: In 1940 the little village of Mardale Green vanished below Haweswater which had been formed into a new reservoir to serve Manchester. In this picture during the drought of 1976 the retreating water has exposed the stone walls and in the centre a bridge from this lost village. (From photos taken by J.O'Ryan).*

THE VILLAGE ELEMENTS
The Church and Parish

After years of stagnation the Church of England sprang into action in the mid 1800s and started to create new churches and parishes to reflect the rapid urban growth. Although most of this work took place in the towns and cities, there were examples in the countryside. For instance in the hill country where the parish had been a long strip running from the village in the valley below, up the slope and onto the plateau above, new parishes and churches were formed to serve the settlements that had now grown up in the upland area.

154

■ *FIG 5.7: LITTLEWICK GREEN, BERKS: A medieval-style church built in 1893 and typical of many Victorian edifices which appeared all over the country.*

This Victorian period also saw a vigorous spate of church restorations which saved many from collapse but also destroyed some ancient architectural features. The process of restoration would usually include removing any outer covering to expose the building material beneath. Mixes of different stones, brick, flint etc may look rustic and charming today but its builders had never intended it to be on show, a bit like removing the brick from your house to show off its breezeblock core! This was a period of Gothic revival, so the styles of medieval architecture were repeated in the new doors, windows, stained glass and decoration used. This can make dating of features tricky to all but the expert eye, though usually the sharply defined edges of window mouldings and the clearly 19th century style of artwork can help to separate it from earlier work.

The Catholic Emancipation Act of 1829 paved the way for new churches to be erected. Edifices from humble Gothic churches up to Westminster Cathedral were built for Catholic worship rather than the private chapels and rooms which had sufficed while anti-papal feelings were still strong. New Nonconformist chapels continued to be built in the 19th century, the Baptists and Methodists (the latter had split into the Wesleyans and Primitives) probably erected the most. Classic facades gave way in the mid and later 1800s to Gothic styles as with their Anglican rivals. Despite all this religious vigour, only about half the population in the 19th century attended church, a decline which in modern times has seen numerous smaller chapels become homes or offices.

Along with the changes in local government and the birth of County Councils, civil parishes were formed in 1889 to administer matters in the village. It is the boundaries of these secular bodies which is marked on Ordnance Survey maps and not the earlier ecclesiastic ones. In a lot of cases the two boundaries will match as these new civil parishes were laid out to reflect the separate areas of poor law administration which had been done within the ecclesiastical parish since its introduction in the 16th century. Larger parishes though were often split up after the 1662 Act of Settlement into smaller areas of poor law administration and it is these vills and townships and not the earlier parish which can form the civil parishes today. Therefore it would be advisable to use the earliest large scale Ordnance Survey maps in establishing and identifying features on these ancient boundaries.

■ *FIG 5.8: WADDESDON, BUCKS: This glorious French chateau-style mansion was built in the late 19th century for Baron Ferdinand de Rothschild, from a banking family who also bought up six other properties in the same area. They were attracted not only by the easy access to London but also by the excellent hunting to be had in the Aylesbury Vale.*

156

Manor Houses and Mansions

The Victorian gentry and aristocrats were just as enthusiastic house builders as their Georgian predecessors. They erected huge Gothic, Italianate, Baronial, French and Classical mansions, often on the site of an earlier and now unfashionable house while some new buildings especially for those who had made their money from industry and finance appeared on a fresh site. Gardens and parks changed most notably with the introduction of new species of trees and shrubs from around the Empire and also by reinterpreting older styles which saw a return of a less open and more compartmented design.

The 20th century break up of these estates saw many mansions converted into schools, hotels, military camps and offices while others were left to become ruins or have been built upon. Some are now under the guardianship of the National Trust while most of the other survivors have had to open to the public to make ends meet, often with additional attractions like safari parks, museums and gardens. The parkland which once surrounded them has often been eaten away by agriculture, plantations, housing estates and road schemes. Single mature trees scattered in a field of corn, rhododendrons, exotic trees and avenues in woodland and perhaps even the odd folly or grotto can indicate a reduced or even vanished estate.

Castles

The castle became fashionable again in the 19th century with the ones that had survived being further embellished with domestic features. Completely new mansions were built in either a Scottish Baronial style with numerous turrets or simply in the form of a mock castle usually with banks of large windows and with a symmetrical front. Some of these, now in ruins, which may look like ancient castles turn out to be less than two hundred years old.

Schools

Although there was an increasing number of village schools being founded by benevolent lords, religious groups and the Church of England in the 19th century, it was the Education Act of 1870 from which most of them date. All over the country brick and stone buildings were erected, often with a date stone from the 1870s. These elementary schools taught children the basics up to a maximum age of thirteen, although most left earlier and attendance could be patchy especially at harvest time. The system whereby village children would only receive their education from a single elementary school lasted in many parts up until the last war, despite the modern system of primary and secondary education having being phased in from 1926.

Inns and Pubs

Inns continued to be built in the 19th century, but now more often to serve railway passengers as well as the road traveller. In the 20th century as the motorways directed traffic away from the main roads and railways closed, the inns which relied on them often had to close too, unless they were able to diversify by becoming more of a pub and restaurant or survive by being in a popular tourist location.

The village tavern and alehouses, or what we now broadly term a pub, reached their peak in numbers in the 19th century although these could still be just a single room serving home brew. Larger, permanent public houses were established either in new or old buildings with a publican or victualler serving beer from two bars, the public with its games and gossip for the workers and the saloon fitted with superior furniture and a piano for the better dressed clientele. These were often used as an outlet of beer for a small local brewery which itself may have been an important employer in your village, and some of its buildings may still exist.

■ FIG 5.9: STOKE LYNE, OXON: This humble pub, which has a central bar behind the window with the stickers and a small public room either side, is a rare surviving example of a real village local as it would have been in the 19th and early 20th century.

In the 20th century the number of drinking houses dropped although the remaining pubs are likely to be larger than their predecessors. Since the war smaller family breweries have been bought out with the dependent pubs either being forced to close or changing to suit the new owners, while the publican has become full time and has had to adapt to a wider social mix of clients and the drinks they demand. In recent decades the armies of visitors to the countryside have increasingly relied on the pub to provide food and cater for the family. The type and quantity of pubs in your village today, whether they have a public bar or are just a restaurant, can be a barometer of the social content of the community.

Shops

Prior to the 19th century most villagers either grew their own food or bought it from the weekly market. Similarly, any goods they required were either made at home or purchased from the craftsmen in the village, while special and exotic items could be bought at the annual fair. As markets declined, and villagers deprived of much of their land became less self sufficient, the shop appeared with the introduction of the penny post in 1841 giving it the additional role of post office.

The 20th century was not kind to the village shop with newcomers to the community being more mobile and able to purchase their food from local towns. The invention of the car and the freezer have a lot to answer for! To survive shops have diversified, selling all manner of goods, local crafts and paintings and like the pub their success or failure can reflect the type of village which they now serve.

Greens and Village Halls

As mentioned in Chapter 2, many so-called greens are recent in origin. In most 19th century planned estate villages the green was seen as a centrepiece to the creators of the romantic composition, while in industrial settlements it was set out with communal and sports activities in mind. In existing villages a new piece of land may have been purchased or granted to the parish, often rectangular and perhaps more of a sports field than a traditional green. Unfortunately many ancient greens were not only built upon in past centuries but also lost or greatly reduced in size when the parish was enclosed. So when looking at your village do not assume that just because there is no green today that there is not one buried under houses or fields which maps and road names can help you identify. Equally be careful not to assume that a present green is automatically ancient especially if it is of a regular shape (most ancient greens are irregular or long thin strips) and surrounded by 19th and 20th century housing or fields.

■ FIG 5.10: TISSINGTON, DERBYSHIRE: A village hall.

Most village halls date from the last hundred years after the formation of parish councils. Some are earlier especially in estate villages where they were provided along with the communal package of church, school and water pump. It seems sacrilege today to think that some of activities which take place in the hall like jumble, plant and cake sales had their medieval equivalent held within the church itself!

Village Pump

The vast majority of village pumps were provided in the 19th century and are of the familiar dome topped, cast iron variety, being very much a product of the industrial age. Some were presented to the village by the local lord or philanthropist and usually bear his name and a date. As mains water was laid on in the 20th century they became redundant and are rarely working today. There are many other curiosities which have been gifted to villages, for instance close by where I live there is an Indian-style well, the figurehead from a ship and a lonely barometer set in a wall. The stories attached to these can link them with national events and figures and make fascinating reading in any village history.

■ *FIG 5.11:*
HAMBLEDEN, BUCKS:
A typical 19th century
village pump.

Houses

With the advent of the railways and new manufacturing processes, previously small scale and locally produced building products became available on a nationwide scale, heralding the demise of vernacular architecture. It became increasingly difficult for village brickworks, quarries and thatchers to compete with these cheaper mass produced goods, so houses made from local stone, timber and straw could give way to bricks from Bedfordshire and slate from North Wales.

In the lowland regions in the 19th century timber-framed houses were now rarely built, only appearing in estate villages for their picturesque value or in the hovels of the very poor. Walls made of a mix of clay and straw continued to be erected in parts of Devon, the Midlands and the North West but here again mainly for basic housing. Stone is still used today from local or distant quarries especially in the upland regions, but in less quantity than before and often only as a facing material. The new mass produced bricks were cheaper and required less preparation and maintenance, so for the first time all over the country new mansions, chapels, houses, cottages, barns and factories were made from the same material irrespective of region. They even found their way into the existing houses, replacing wattle and daub as an infill in timber-framed houses and even as an outer layer on some clay and straw houses.

The wide availability of slate in the 19th century transformed the roofs of England as the new brick houses were usually topped with a grey crown. As slate is lighter than other materials the pitch of the roof can be shallower and this is a distinctive feature of houses in the 19th century, although older houses were also re-roofed in it, sometimes maintaining the previous steeper pitch, other times lowering it. Just as slate in the 1800s put thatchers out of business, mass produced roof tiles in the 1900s has forced the abandonment of slate quarries and mines as well as their associated settlements and railways.

The houses lower down the village social ladder started to reflect the latest in architectural fashions in the 19th century whether it be Classical, Gothic, or Arts and Crafts. This makes it easier to date houses in your village from this period although it took a number of years for a style which was popular in London to spread to the more rural and distant parts of the country. The choice of bonding

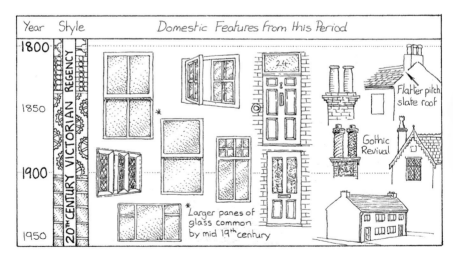

■ FIG 5.12: A chart showing some of the styles of domestic architectural features from this period although with the rapidly changing fashions of the 20th century many reappear.

162

for the brickwork, for instance 'rat bond' was used in the early 19th century to reduce the brick tax paid, or even the colours of bricks like the mixes of red and yellow which were popular in the 1870s and 80s can also help. Windows, doors, chimneys and detailing like bargeboards can be accurately dated but caution has to be applied as they could be fitted into an older or more recent house. In estate villages the style chosen by the landlord and his architect may reflect some romantic ideal rather than the popular trend of the day and as existing houses would have been rebuilt to match the new it takes an expert eye to correctly date them. In this situation documentary evidence and maps may be a more reliable source of dating.

Despite the availability of these new products vast numbers of the working population of Village England were still living in tiny cottages, hovels and shacks well into the 20th century. It was only then that Government bodies started to erect the council houses for these agricultural workers that still today line roads or form estates in the periphery of the village. These must have seemed like mansions to the first families moving into them! Another important development of the last century was the provision of mains water, sewerage and electricity. It is so often forgotten how very recently in historic terms villagers were walking miles to collect water, suffering with insanitary conditions and working by oil lamp and candlelight.

TRANSPORT
Roads
By the early 19th century more than 20,000 miles of roads were maintained by the Turnpike Trusts but their profits were eroded by canals and then critically by the railways. Most had gone out of business by 1880, the last one in 1895, with their responsibilities passing over to local government. Despite the influence of the Turnpike Trusts the majority of roads were still little more than tracks without defined edges which were repaired by members of the parish. In 1835 the system changed to one where a rate was levied on the parish for their maintenance and surveyors for the highways were appointed. The improved drainage and new methods of surfacing slowly filtered down to lesser roads but neatly edged modern tarmac ones only developed in the last 70 or so years as the car heralded a new boom time for our highways.

The 18th and 19th century turnpike roads were often straight like the enclosure roads of the same date and both can be mistaken for Roman ones, a situation which is further confused as some followed these ancient routes. In the 20th century major engineering works like new bridges, cuttings and embankments further relegated parts of old routes though these can still be found as parking spaces and tracks alongside many of them. Another place where the course of a main road may have changed is where it climbs a hill, with a number of progressively straighter routes of shallower gradient found beside each other. The most influential in the last century has been the by-pass. Although it can bring peace to the roadside inhabitants, the loss of passing traffic can ruin a shop or garage's business, while the land now enclosed by the by-pass is an easy target for the house developer. A centuries-old settlement which lived off the traveller can easily become just another dormitory village.

Railways

After the opening of the Stockton and Darlington and Liverpool to Manchester railways the potential of these new iron horses was realised and in an incredibly short time a massive network spread across the countryside. The speed and versatility of the railway quickly extinguished the canals and turnpike roads and transformed the villages which they served. Not only could passengers travel to towns and cities they had previously had only heard about, but the urban folk could visit the countryside as the speed of the train made the daytrip a possibility in a time before holidays. More important was the improved transportation of goods from the village like milk, livestock, grain, fish, fruit and vegetables which could now reach their destinations while still fresh. Natural commodities from the locality like stone, coal, timber, clays, lime and slate and products from iron and steel down to beer and whisky could be moved in quantity to an expanding worldwide market bringing increased profits to landlord, factory owner and farmer. At the same time the trains could also bring coal into the village, possibly ending the coppicing of trees in your local woods which had previously been the main source of fuel. Although the arrival of a railway brought prosperity to many lowland regions, it was in the industrial, fishing and upland farming communities that the benefits were really felt with a rapid expansion from hamlets into villages and even towns.

In turn though the railways fixed to rigid routes and minimum viable loads could not compete with the more versatile road transport and from as early as the 1930s lines started to close. The Beeching Report of 1963 led to the sudden closing of a fifth of railways and a third of stations nationwide, though those which survived this threat are probably still running today. Discovering lost railway lines and more importantly the stations and goods loading areas can reveal which products were being transported and therefore what the landscape around could have looked like then and how it affected the village's development.

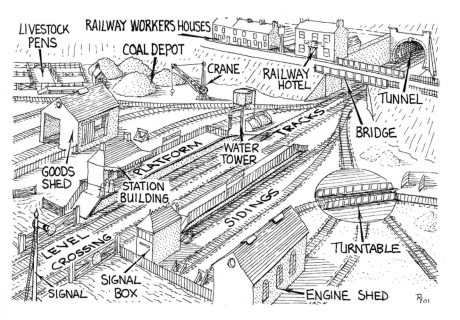

■ *FIG 5.13: A view showing the main features which you may be able to recognise around an existing or disused railway line today.*

THE VILLAGERS

As villages by the 19th century had developed into specific types rather than being primarily agricultural, the social structure of these rural communities does not fit into any neat generalisation. Whether your village was an open, unregulated settlement with Nonconformist chapels or was a closed estate one where the Church of England was more influential will affect who lived there. Fortunately with the advent of the census in 1801 and numerous trade directories it is increasingly easy to identify the make up of your village.

The lord could still be a major aristocrat, a gentleman or a squire although successful industrialists and capitalists were frequently purchasing their estates and joining this class. Some were absent from what may have been just one of many estates they owned while others took an active interest in their agricultural and industrial development. Most though enjoyed hunting which was still the major pastime for the gentry and some of the new middle classes.

In addition to fox hunting, developments in the gun had made shooting popular, with woodland and copses being retained and laid out for the breeding of birds like pheasants especially in the agricultural depressions of 1820-40 and 1870-

1900. At the time of the shoot men would drive the birds out of the trees towards the gunmen standing in the surrounding fields. The control, protection and breeding of game animals and birds was the responsibility of the gamekeeper, the huntsman looked after the fox hounds, while the Master of the Hunt, who may have been the lord himself, had overall control of the pack. Other members of staff on a Victorian estate included gardeners, coachmen, butlers, maids and cooks. Although the lord would have little contact with the peasantry now, his lavish lifestyle and estate farms still provided most of the employment in the dependent settlement.

This is the age when full time professionals took over some of the roles which were previously unpaid or part time. The local vicar, rector or minister would have been among the most important along with the farmers, then the schoolmasters or mistresses, parish clerks and constables, doctors and apothecaries. Along with them were the various tradesmen like blacksmiths, wheelwrights, carpenters, builders, butchers, bakers, grocers, tailors, cobblers, tanners, millers and

■ *FIG 5.14: BLACK COUNTRY MUSEUM, WEST MIDLANDS: A busy canalside scene which could date from any time in the 19th century. The boatmen and their family living on board boats like these is a popular image, but originally when times were good they only worked on them and had a house and family elsewhere. It was only the decline of waterways traffic which forced them to make their boat a home as well.*

publicans. If there was a local industry then there could be iron workers, miners, quarrymen, brickmakers and masons. The transport of their goods would necessitate a stationmaster, signalman and workers on the railways, a gatekeeper, surveyor and roadmen on the turnpikes, while on the canals there were wharfingers, lock-keepers, lengthsmen and boatmen. Despite all these jobs perhaps half of the villagers in the early 1800s were farm labourers, the professionals only becoming more numerous later on in the century with the agricultural depression.

■ FIG 5.15: GREAT TEW, OXON: This seemingly timeless village of rustic stone cottages is not all it seems. It is primarily the creation of 19th century lords who remodelled existing houses, built new ones in a similar rustic manner, enlarged their own house and its lands, laid out new roads including an early by-pass, and created the small green. Despite its undeniable beauty Great Tew was a village in decline with cottages and farms being left in ruin until the ban on outsiders buying up properties was lifted as recently as the 1980s.

The 20th century saw the decline and extinction of so many of the above roles from the landlord down to the humble labourer. Those that have survived have adapted to the changing times, blacksmiths for example becoming more mobile to service the horse riding and equestrian business, while other craftsmen produce goods for tourists rather than villagers. Farmers diversify by offering bed and breakfast, selling off barns for conversion and turning over land for Sunday markets, fishing lakes and other leisure activities. The village at the dawn of the 21st century has yet again adapted to a changing environment, most being dominated for the first time by the middle classes, with those working the land being in the minority.

■ *FIG 5.16: HALTON, BUCKS: A row of houses which were built or remodelled in the 1870s when this estate village was developed by another member of the Rothschild family (see fig 5.8 - page 156). The black and white timber frame above red brickwork, the decorative bargeboards and elaborate Tudor-style chimneys were popular from this period through to the early 20th century. In 1918 this estate was purchased by the RAF and new barracks and housing estates have transformed the village yet again.*

CONCLUSION

As I compare the area around my home today to a map drawn less than two hundred years ago I can see changes in all the villages. Many have been affected by enclosure and drainage schemes, while in others new houses built by benevolent landlords have transformed agricultural settlements. In some the arrival of the Army and Airforce with new barracks, housing, chapels and shops has dwarfed the original hamlet, while quarrying in others has vastly expanded their size. Nearly all of these villages though have been affected by the coming of the railway and then the motorway, both of which still encourage commuting and have resulted in new estates, barn conversions and the modernising of old cottages.

I can therefore clearly see the effects which the Industrial Age has had around me and it is all too easy to hark back to the good old days when we assume traditional village life was unchanging. One thing though I have learnt myself from researching this book is that this never was the case. Villages have always changed due to agriculture, the actions of its lord, local or national industries and passing trade. What is different is

the rapid speed of these changes in the 20th century.

It is also clear from looking at my local villages that it is impossible to generalise about their development. There are ones built to serve an estate, a number based around an old triangular green, another stretched along an old turnpike road, three built around RAF and Army camps and at least four deserted villages. Despite similarities due to local geology each one is individual and if tracing the history of your village be careful not to assume it grew for the same reasons or in the same way as its neighbour.

The other question I pondered over in the introduction was whether villages grew naturally in a gradual and random manner. I was surprised to find that most were partly or fully planned at some stage, even in the Middle Ages when they developed to suit the open field system. It is also astonishing to find that thousands of them have since declined and disappeared even into the 20th century. There are far fewer villages today than in 1300 and a greater proportion of the population are urban dwellers so it could be argued that villages have been in decline ever since the catastrophes of the 14th century!

Saxon invaders may have played their part in the development of villages, but it was the incoming people from the towns and cities who in the 20th century, for better or worse, addressed their physical decline. Perhaps only because of an English love for the rustic or as a reaction to the rapidly changing urban environment, most of us who have been brought up in towns aspire to live in or at least visit these tranquil idylls. And it has been this decision to keep, protect and treasure the unique heritage locked up in our villages that has ensured the survival of many in the face of declining rural employment.

STILL THERE
FEATURES TO LOOK OUT FOR

■ *FIG 5.17: HAMPTON GAY, OXON: A village which has now almost disappeared. The settlement declined despite its close proximity to Oxford with the stone manor house in the picture being abandoned after a fire in 1887. All that really remains today isolated at the end of a dead end lane is the old church and the Manor Farm.*

■ FIG 5.18: LOWER SLAUGHTER, GLOS: An early 19th century water mill which has retained its wheel despite the presence of a chimney indicating a steam engine which would normally have replaced it. In one of the most picturesque of the Cotswold villages this industrial building serves as a reminder that not only were they up until recently working settlements but also that most of these villages developed around the wool industry.

■ FIG 5.19:
AVONCROFT
MUSEUM OF
HISTORIC
BUILDINGS: A late
19th century chapel
clad in corrugated
iron. These were
typically built to
serve isolated
communities or
smaller religious
groups and can still
be found today all
over the country.

■ *FIG 5.20: WEALD AND DOWNLAND OPEN AIR MUSEUM: A distinctive long, open-sided drying shed of the type that were a feature in local brickworks throughout the 19th and early 20th century. The freshly shaped bricks were stacked under here to dry, before being fired in a kiln.*

■ *FIG 5.21: WEALD AND DOWNLAND OPEN AIR MUSEUM: Hexagonal or round buildings like this can be found attached to the side of farm buildings or freestanding. They were used to contain a horse fixed to an arm with the animal walking round endlessly in circles powering a crushing or mixing device or, if linked to another building, turning the machinery within it. This one is a 19th century pugmill where the raw clay was worked into a paste in the brickmaking process.*

■ FIG 5.22: AVONCROFT MUSEUM OF HISTORIC BUILDINGS: A collection of Victorian brick chimneys in a Tudor style, although the original 16th century ones they were imitating would not have been topped with a pot and their brickwork would be more worn and less consistent. The chimney pots like the ones in the foreground had been introduced in the late 18th century to improve the draw on the fire below.

■ FIG 5.23: SHELDON, DERBYSHIRE: An old lead mine with a ruined engine house and its chimney to the left.

■ *FIG 5.24: EWELME, OXON: In the villages blessed with clear chalk streams, cress beds like these were a common feature in the 19th and 20th centuries, although most are now disused and overgrown.*

■ *FIG 5.25: BISHOPSTONE, WILTS: A late Victorian Primitive Methodist chapel, with a date of 1886 around the startling circular window.*

■ *FIG 5.26: DOWNLEY COMMON, BUCKS: Although many commons were divided up at the time of enclosure there are still some survivors today like this example in the Chilterns where animals still graze unbounded by fences.*

CHAPTER 6
TRACING THE HISTORY OF YOUR VILLAGE

■ *FIG 6.1: Features around your village to look out for and record before researching its history.*

The first thing to decide upon before researching is to what degree you are going to trace the history of your village. Are you intending to look at the whole picture or are you more interested in just the social or physical side? Perhaps you want to concentrate on one particular feature, place or person, or on a particular period in history. If you intend to produce a book at the end of the project you may wish to approach publishers of similar local works or look at the costs of printing it yourself before commencing. You also may wish to team up with someone else or even work as a group.

When researching it is important to keep good notes, recording sources of material, taping conversations with local people and indexing all your information. You will frequently find that something that seemed unimportant at the time can later prove to be the missing part of a jigsaw and the easier it is to retrieve it the better. The County Library and Records Office will be your second home for the duration of your research! Most of the information you will ever require is held here and although bewildering at first help is always at hand. If the thought of sifting through pages of old documents puts you off then you can probably still do a fairly good job from the books which are available by experts who have done this backbreaking work for you. Finally do not feel you have to be an expert historian or archaeologist to take on this task. There are so many books, TV programmes, internet sites, evening classes and museums available to the enthusiastic amateur that with an open minded approach and, most of all, time and patience you can achieve your goal.

Before burying your head in books and documents I would suggest starting by spending some time walking around the village and surrounding fields and familiarising yourself with features and names. Fig 6.1 lists some of the things to look out for and note on a map or your own plan. Having a first hand knowledge of the area will make research a whole lot easier and it also may help identify some features which will be worthy of more detailed investigation.

The first section of the list below comprises some of the sources of information which should be found in your County Library or Records Office and are generally easy to access and understand:

EXISTING LOCAL HISTORIES

If there is already a book published about your village it will be worth reading, although try and digest the facts rather than the opinions of the author as your interpretation of documents may differ. Do not let its presence put you off your own project. Many of these books only record tales from those still living so you could concentrate on the more distant past while others may have been written some time ago and could benefit from new sources of information and modern thinking on the subject.

COUNTY HISTORY BOOKS

In addition to local studies there will also be a number of history books covering your county which may have additional information on your village and can also be useful in showing where your settlement fitted into the local picture. For instance the flow of traffic through my old village is north to south towards the nearest present town, but this it turned out had only sprung up in Victorian times around a new railway station. In reading the county history I found the nearest market before this was in a different direction which explained why the older houses in the village were aligned on a west to east axis and that what is now just a track was once the main road to this town.

Some of these county histories can date back to the 19th or even earlier centuries. Although their interpretation of ancient remains is dubious in the light of modern work, the facts they contain about what was then recent history can be invaluable.

THE VICTORIA HISTORY OF THE COUNTIES OF ENGLAND

From 1899 work started on a series of books to cover the history of every parish in every county of England. A hundred years on and the work is still continuing; some counties are complete with others only partly and a few have no published volumes at all. If you are fortunate your parish will appear in one of the volumes held at your County Library and sometimes locally and will include the local geology and a history of the manors, estates, churches and industry in and around your village. Remember though that some of these volumes were written early in the last century and they may not cover the topics you are interested in and some of their conclusions may be outdated.

LITERATURE

There are fiction and non fiction books written in the past which are very good at adjusting your mind to everyday life in a certain period. These can range from the classics like Chaucer's *Canterbury Tales*, written in the 14th century, to the stories of country folk like Flora Thompson's *Lark Rise to Candleford*, written about life in the late 1800s.

ARCHITECTURAL BOOKS

Dating and understanding the development of buildings in your village will be important and thankfully there are a number of books and sources which can help the novice. The most impressive is the *Buildings of England* series mainly written by Sir Nicholas Pevsner in the 1950s and 60s. These popular books on each county are constantly being updated and are an authoritative guide to the local architecture. Pevsner was, however, looking at the village with a critical eye and old buildings of no true architectural merit may have been overlooked. I also recommend *Tracing the History of Houses* by B.Breckon, J.Parker and M.Andrew.

Another important source is the guide to the local listed buildings, which should be found in the County Library. This should list every old or important building with its appropriate grade, along with a short piece on its date and origin. There are other books worth consulting on regional architecture but these will tend to concentrate only on major houses and the parish church.

RECORDS OF COUNTY ARCHAEOLOGICAL GROUPS
Your County Library or local museum should hold the records of regional archaeology groups. My local one publishes a new book every year with reports from the latest digs down to the most minor of finds and its back catalogue dates from the mid 19th century. Most counties also have some form of Monuments Record which contains maps, aerial photographs and surveys of historic sites in the county.

CENSUS
From 1801 a national census has been held every ten years with the exception of 1941. Vital information can be obtained not only from the personal records and family names but also by studying population numbers and local professions.

TRADE DIRECTORIES
Lists of professionals and importantly the place they worked within your parish, dating back to the 19th century.

MAPS
Since the turn of the 19th century the Ordnance Survey has been responsible for accurately mapping the country and the earliest of the large scale maps are a great source of information not only in how your village has developed but also in recording features which have since been destroyed. The library should hold copies while you can buy your own from Ordnance Survey agents and other outlets. From the 16th until the 19th century maps were produced for a local estate, enclosure and tithe awards and travellers. Although the older ones should not be assumed to be accurate they are an excellent source of information and are one of the rare glimpses you may get into the physical appearance of your village in a bygone age.

PHOTOS
There are countless books full of old photographs dating from the mid 19th century, while local individuals and groups may hold other copies. They can be surprisingly useful in dating and understanding structures and buildings from their previous forms, as well as the social and economic state of the village.

NEWSPAPERS AND MAGAZINES
Provincial newspapers appeared in the 18th century and then boomed in the late 19th century. Old copies are usually held on microfiche at the County Library. Old copies of magazines like *Country Life* can be of historic value just as present-day publications like *Current Archaeology* can contain useful research and discoveries.

PLACE AND FIELD NAMES
In the past the place name of a settlement has been used to date its foundation and name the people involved and their country of origin. This was useful as most of our villages appeared in the Saxon period before any records were made. Unfortunately when archaeologists have investigated sites the dates of their finds do not match with that implied by the name of the settlement.

As explained in Chapter 2 the foundation of our villages is far more complex and spread over a greater period than previously thought, so although the translation of the name may be correct it may not have been applied to the nucleated settlement which we see today. The name could be of the estate which an incoming Saxon or Viking had fought for, been rewarded with or simply purchased and it was only at a later date that the farmsteads and hamlets within it formed into the central village which retained the name of the estate. So for instance the name may date from the 7th century, but the village you are interested in might have only been founded with the laying out of the open fields in the 10th century.

The reverse is also possible with a new lord of the manor having an existing village, which may have been standing for centuries, named after him. Perhaps some were even named after important figures or by natives wishing to show respect to incoming invaders, as today there are cities named Victoria all around the old British Empire. It was also usual in recorded times for a Norman family to affix their name to that of an existing settlement especially if it was composed of more than one manor held by different lords. Sometimes the common name is later dropped, leaving just the family name applied to the present village.

Field names can be of great importance and frequently record the presence of an old building or structures, the properties of the land and its previous uses. For instance a mysterious mound which could be a Bronze Age burial turns out to be more recent when you discover it is standing in Windmill Field. These names may be known by the farmer or recorded on old estate, enclosure and tithe award maps.

There are numerous books dedicated to the translation and interpretation of place and field names held within your County Library. The value of the names will depend on what physical remains can be discovered from or associated with them.

The second section of the list includes just some of the important documents that may be of use in your research, copies of which may be held in the County Library or Records Office, at the British Library or with other national groups. It is well worth reading some of the books written by experts in these fields before tackling the documents yourself:

PARISH RECORDS

From the mid 16th until early 19th century the parish was the centre of local organisation and the records maintained are of immense value to the historian. The Parish Register in which christenings, weddings and burials were recorded is the most notable source, but other documents like accounts and records of the Churchwarden, Constable, Overseer of the Poor and Surveyor of Roads may also be enlightening.

ECCLESIASTICAL RECORDS

There are many other documents associated with the church which can prove useful, including records of monasteries and their possessions, Church Courts and the visitations by senior clergymen to the parish.

ESTATE AND MANOR RECORDS

There may be existing documents from the everyday running of the local estate from lists of accounts and the records of the Manor Court, to the renting and selling of land and the surveys and maps associated with it.

GOVERNMENT RECORDS

There have been numerous surveys for information and collections of taxes over the centuries for kings, queens and their governments. The Domesday Book is probably the best known, but others include Hundreds Rolls, Poll Tax, Lay Subsidy Rolls, Hearth Tax and Muster Rolls. The records of these can be fragmentary and it is worth consulting a book or expert about the interpretation of their contents as well as the translation of some of the earlier ones. Judicial records of the various bodies of law also date back to the medieval period.

PERSONAL RECORDS

The most useful of personal records are probably the wills and probate inventories in which were listed the possessions of the deceased, helping to reveal the standard of living of the villagers. It is also worth enquiring to see if any family letters or personal diaries have survived from within the parish.

AERIAL PHOTOGRAPHS

Very useful for spotting archaeological features and for making sense of what may appear as a set of lumps and bumps on the ground. Older photographs which can date back to the 1930s may also be useful in finding features which have since been ploughed over or removed as well as recording the village before later development. Patterns which show up as marks in a field of corn or as shadows and parch marks on grass are not straightforward to interpret and there are books available to help. The best starting point from which to find an aerial photograph of your village and parish is the National Monuments Record Centre (RCHME), Kemble Drive, Swindon, Wilts SN2 2GZ.

Other sources:

FIELDWALKING

The action of the modern plough across a field can bring to the surface artifacts, building material, charcoal and pottery from previous human activity. Many old settlements, farmsteads, industrial workings and burials have been discovered by groups of enthusiasts and archaeologists simply walking systematically across freshly ploughed fields. You obviously need an expert eye and the permission of the farmer, but you may find that a local group have already covered the area and records of their finds are available. Alternatively you may be able to organise fieldwalking with the help of local archaeological groups or professionals.

INTERVIEWING LOCALS

Many local histories are mainly composed of the recollections of older members of the community, while there are useful books by groups like the Women's Institute in which are recorded the everyday lives of villagers in the early 20th century. You can interview locals yourself, especially people who have lived there since childhood or own a particular building you are interested in. Always try and take notes though or ask permission to record the conversations as with all the snippets of information you will pick up, their value may only appear upon a later revelation. The only limitation here is to remember that you are recording the state of the village from probably late Victorian times and that everyday life in the village even fifty years before could have been different.

INTERNET

There is an increasing amount of information which can be accessed from the internet simply by trying the search engines with place names and subjects. I have found that websites for archaeological sites can be very informative while some from even major national bodies can be disappointing at this stage.

HISTORICAL SITES AND RECONSTRUCTIONS

Below I have listed a number of places I visited during the writing of the book which I feel are useful in gaining a greater understanding of how your village may have looked in the past. They also make a very pleasant day out if you are in the area:

West Stow: Site of an Early Saxon village with a number or reconstructed houses. Off the A1101 between Mildenhall and Bury St Edmunds, Suffolk.

Weald and Downland Open Air Museum, Singleton, West Sussex: Impressive collection of timber-framed, brick and stone houses and buildings from medieval to Victorian periods with original exteriors and interiors. An excellent guidebook shows the buildings before reconstruction and how far removed they had become from their original form. Just off the A286 between Midhurst and Chichester.

Avoncroft Museum of Historic Buildings, Bromsgrove, Worcs: Wide selection of buildings including a working windmill. Just off the A38 at Stoke Heath, to the south of Bromsgrove.

Chiltern Open Air Museum, Newlands Park, Gorelands Lane, Chalfont St Giles, Bucks: Collection of buildings from an Iron Age round hut to a prefabricated bungalow. Situated 1 mile east of the A413 at Chalfont St Giles.

GLOSSARY

ANGLICAN: An adjective to describe the Church of England.

ANGLO SAXON: An adjective used to describe the period from the departure of the Romans to the Norman invasion of 1066. It comes from two of the three Germanic groups, the Angles and the Saxons, who arrived in England in the 5th century.

APSE: The semicircular or polygonal end of the chancel, particularly on Saxon and Norman churches and sometimes replicated on Victorian ones.

ASSARTING: From a French word, used in this book for the clearing out of trees for agriculture.

BYRE: In this book it applies to the end of a longhouse where the livestock were kept, although in later farms it is the cow shed.

CAPITAL: The decorative top piece of a column.

CLASSIC: In this book it applies to the styles of building from the 17th-19th centuries which were based on Greek and Roman architecture.

DARK AGES: The term which historians have applied to the 5th-7th century - due to the lack of writing and archaeology, rather than being a period which the people at the time would have been aware of.

DAUB: A varying mixture of mud, clay, straw and other materials applied to the wattle infills in a timber-framed building, or used to cover the entire walls of prehistoric round houses.

DOCTRINE: The principles of a religious belief.

ECCLESIASTICAL: Of the church (see 'Secular').

EDIFICE: A large, imposing building, used in this book for a church.

FACADE: Front or face of a building.

FALLOW: Land which has been ploughed but is left uncultivated for a period of time in order to return nutrients to the soil.

FARMSTEAD: The farm and its buildings.

GOTHIC (from the Germanic tribe, the Goths): The period of medieval architecture where the pointed arch was used - reappeared in the late 18th and 19th century.

HAMLET: A small settlement of approximately 3 to 19 households (see 'Village').

HEARTH: Used in this book for the area on the floor where the fire was in a house or hall before the development of the fireplace.

HEATHEN: In this book it refers to people who were not Christian.

HOLLOWAY: A road or track where constant wear has formed a cutting.

HUNTER GATHERERS: Pre farming age peoples who lived by hunting animals and gathering fruits etc. In this book it refers to the Middle Stone Age people from the end of the last Ice Age up until the coming of agriculture, in the New Stone Age, sometime around 4500 BC.

HUSBANDRY: The word used to describe farming especially in the books and literature of the 16th and 17th centuries. Probably best described as caring and nurturing the land rather than the later farming for a profit.

LINEAR: Something set in a line, or narrow and long in shape.

LONGHOUSE: Literally a long house, which in this book is applied to the single-storey style of peasant house with the family living at one end and their livestock at the other. A very typical medieval type which can still be found in some upland regions and Scotland.

LYCHGATE: Usually a wooden frame with a roof at the entrance to the churchyard where the coffin was rested before being summoned into the church by the clergyman.

MANOR: An estate under the feudal control of a lord. The building from where the estate was administered and in which the lord usually lived was the Manor House.

MERE: In this context it refers to a lake (particularly in Cheshire and Shropshire) which was formed by melted blocks of ice which have been covered by later deposits.

MESOLITHIC: Middle Stone Age, used in this book to describe the period between the end of the last Ice Age and about 4500 BC (also 'Hunter Gatherers').

NEOLITHIC: New Stone Age, used in this book to describe the period from when the first farmers arrived, around 4500 BC, up until bronze tools appeared, around 2500 BC.

OPPIDUM: The word used by Julius Caesar to describe a type of small town which he found when invading Britain in 55-54 BC.

PALING: A fence made from vertical timbers.

PHILANTHROPIST: Someone who cares for the welfare of mankind, usually through an act of benevolence.

POLITE ARCHITECTURE: Used in this book to describe elegant and refined houses which were built with materials from outside the locality (used as an opposite to 'Vernacular').

REEVE: An administrator of land used by Saxon and Norman kings to enforce their rule. The Shire Reeve became known as a Sheriff.

RENAISSANCE: In this book used to refer to the revival of art in 14th-16th century Europe and the style of architecture which developed from it.

ROOD: A Saxon word for a crucifix.

SECULAR: In this book used to describe buildings and organisations concerned with matters of the state, as opposed to ecclesiastical matters of the church.

SINK HOLES: Depressions sometimes later filled with water, which have been caused by acidic water dissolving the alkaline rock (usually limestone) around an existing joint or fault.

TITHING/TOWNSHIP: An ancient secular administrative area as opposed to the parish which was the ecclesiastical one. These areas were usually known as a tithing in the south of the country and as a township or 'vill' in the north.

TRUSSES: A framework placed across a building to support the main roof timbers.

VERNACULAR: Used in this book to refer to houses built from local materials by local craftsmen.

VILLAGE: Referred to as a settlement of 20 or more households but without the administrative trappings of a town, but the boundaries between a village and a smaller hamlet are vague.

VILL: An ancient secular administrative area (see 'Township').

WATTLE: The weavework of thin branches used to make walls between timbers, then covered in daub (hence wattle and daub).

BIBLIOGRAPHY

The dates given are those of the last revision that I used.

GENERAL BOOKS:

Michael Aston: *Interpreting the Landscape: Landscape Archaeology and Local History*, 1985
Michael Aston, David Austin and Christopher Dyer (Editors): *The Rural Settlements of Medieval England*, 1989
Simon Fowler: *Starting Out in Local History*, 2001
Juliet Gardiner and Neil Wenborn (Editors): *The History Today Companion to British History*, 1995
W.G. Hoskins: *Local History in England*, 1984
David Iredale and John Barrett: *Discovering Local History*, 1999
Richard Muir: *Shell Guide to Reading the Landscape*, 1981
Richard Muir: *The Villages of England*, 1992
Richard Muir: *Portraits of the Past*, 1989
Oliver Rackham: *The Illustrated History of the Countryside*, 1994
Trevor Rowley: *Villages in the Landscape*, 1978
Ron Scholes: *Understanding the Countryside: Man's Impact on the Landscape*, 1985
Roy Strong: *The Story of Britain*, 1996
Christopher Taylor: *Village and Farmstead*, 1983
Joan Thirsk (Editor): *The English Rural Landscape*, 2000
Kate Tiller: *An Introduction to English Local History*, 1992
G. Young: *Country Eye*, 1991

BOOKS COVERING A SPECIFIC PERIOD:

Frank Barlow: *The Feudal Kingdom of England*, 1988
Guy de la Bedoyere: *Book of Roman Villas and the Countryside*
Richard Britnell (Editor): *Daily Life in the Later Middle Ages*, 1998
Ken Dark and Petra Dark: *The Landscape of Roman Britain*, 1997
Timothy Darvill: *Prehistoric Britain*, 1987
James Dyer: *Ancient Britain*, 1990
Alan Harding: *England in the 13th Century*, 1993
Peter Hunter Blair: *Anglo/Saxon England*, 1977
Robert Jackson: *Dark Age Britain*, 1984
Maurice Keen: *English Society in the Later Middle Ages*, 1990
R.J. Mercer: *Causewayed Enclosures*, 1990
R.I. Page: *Life in Anglo Saxon England*, 1970

Michael Parker Pearson: *Bronze Age Britain*, 1993
Julian Richards: *Viking Age Britain*, 1991
Alison Weir: *The Wars of the Roses*, 1995
Martin Welch: *Book of Anglo-Saxon England*, 1992
Philip Ziegler: *The Black Death*, 1969

ARCHITECTURE:
R. Allen Brown: *English Castles*, 1976
John Anthony: *Discovering Period Gardens*, 1997
David Austin, Mac Dowdy and Judith Miller: *Be Your Own House Detective*, 1997
Mervyn Blatch: *Parish Churches of England in Colour*, 1974
Bill Breckon and Jeffrey Parker: *Tracing the History of Houses*, 2000
R.W. Brunskill: *Brick Buildings in Britain*, 1990
R.W. Brunskill: *Traditional Farm Buildings of Britain*
R.W. Brunskill: *Houses and Cottages of Britain*, 1997
Lyndon F. Cave: *The Smaller English House*, 1981
Richard Harris: *Discovering Timber Framed Buildings*, 1979
Nigel Harvey: *Old Farm Buildings*, 1987
Richard Hayman: *Church Misericords and Bench Ends*, 1989
Gwyn Headley and Wim Meulenkamp: *Follies, Grottos and Garden Buildings*, 1999
David Iredale and John Barrett: *Discovering Your Old House*, 1991
Brian Kemp: *Church Monuments*, 1985
Nicholas Pevsner: *The Buildings Of England series*, (Most counties covered, many in conjunction with other authors)
Colin Platt: *The Parish Churches of Medieval England*, 1981
Warwick Rodwell: *The Archaeology of the English Church*, 1981
Patricia and Bruce Robertson: *Buildings of Britain*, 1992
Peter Ryder: *Bastle Houses in the Northern Pennines*, 1996
Christopher Taylor: *Parks and Gardens of Britain*, 1998
Margaret Wood: *The English Medieval House*, 1965

INDUSTRY AND TRANSPORT:
Martin Cook: *Medieval Bridges*, 1998
Martin Hammond: *Bricks and Brickmaking*, 1990
Geoffrey Hayes: *Coal Mining*, 2000
Edward Paget-Tomlinson: *The Illustrated History of Canal and River Navigations*, 1993
Peter Stanier: *Quarries and Quarrying*, 1985
Christopher Taylor: *Roads and Tracks of Britain*, 1994
David Turnock: *Railways in the British Isles: Landscape, Land Use and Society*, 1982

AGRICULTURE, BOUNDARIES, ARCHAEOLOGY AND GEOLOGY:
Mark Bowden (Editor): *Unravelling the Landscape: An Inquisitive Approach to Archaeology,* 1999
Denis Britton: *Agriculture in Britain: Changing Pressures and Policies,* 1990
Andrew Goudie: *Landforms of England and Wales,* 1990
Brian Lee: *Fields and Hedgerows - A Nature Guide,* 1985
Ian Simmons and Michael Tooley (Editors): *The Environment in British Prehistory,* 1981
Christopher Taylor: *Fields in the English Landscape,* 2000
Angus Winchester: *Discovering Parish Boundaries,* 2000
Nigel Woodcock: *Geology and Environment in Britain and Ireland,* 1994

INDEX